Away from Home

Quilts inspired by the Lowell factory girls

BY NANCY AND OLIVER RINK

EDITOR: Donna di Natale
DESIGNER: Brian Grubb
PHOTOGRAPHY: Aaron T. Leimkuehler
ILLUSTRATION: Lon Eric Craven
TECHNICAL EDITOR: Christina DeArmond
PRODUCTION ASSISTANCE: Jo Ann Groves

Published by: KANSAS CITY STAR BOOKS

1729 Grand Blvd., Kansas City, Missouri, USA 64108

All rights reserved
Copyright © 2012 Nancy and Oliver Rink and The Kansas City Star Co.

No part of this book may be reproduced, stored in a retrieval system, or transmitted in any form or by any means, electronic, mechanical, photocopying, recording or otherwise, without the prior consent of the publisher. Exception: we grant permission to photocopy the patterns on pages 81-104 for personal use only.

First edition, second printing
ISBN: 9781611690422

Library of Congress Control Number: 2012933896

Printed in the United States of America by Walsworth Publishing Co., Marceline, MO

To order copies, call StarInfo at (816) 234-4636 and say "Books."

PickleDish.com
The Quilter's Home Page

KANSAS CITY STAR QUILTS
Continuing the Tradition

www.PickleDish.com

Dedication

Song of the Spinners

The day is o'er, nor longer we toil and spin;
For ev'ning's hush withdraws from the daily din,
And now we sing, with gladsome hearts,
The theme of the spinner's song,
That labor to leisure a zest imparts,
Unknown to the idle throng.

We spin all day, and then,
In the time for rest,
Sweet peace is found,
A joyous and welcome guest.
Despite of toil we all agree,
Or out of the Mills, or in,
Dependent on others we ne'er will be,
So long as we're able to spin.

from the Lowell Offering, 1841

Away From Home
Quilts inspired by the Lowell factory girls

Table of Contents

About the Authors

Nancy Rink is an award-winning quilter and pattern designer. The year 2004 was a very big year for Nancy. In April 2004 she was the featured artist at the Best of the Valley Quilt Show in Tulare, California. Bobbie Moore, the show's organizer, was quoted in the *Bakersfield Californian* saying, "Rink's work is especially unusual. She's an appliqué artist and her stitches are almost invisible, they're exquisite. She makes beautiful use of color and motion in her work." At the 2004 Houston International Quilt Festival, *Remembrance of Nanny* and *Desert Star* were both given Honorable Mentions. Also in 2004, *Dogtooth Violets* earned one of the top awards in the Kaufman Quilt Quest. Nancy has won awards at other national shows including the Pacific International Quilt Festival, the Pennsylvania National Quilt Extravaganza, the Mid-Atlantic Quilt Festival and the Indiana Heritage Quilt Show. Her medallion-style quilt *Desert Star* was awarded first place in the 2002 From the Mills Contest and was on display at the American Textile History Museum in Lowell, Massachusetts.

After twenty-three years of teaching junior high and high school English, Nancy is now a professional quilter and pattern designer. She still remembers her first experience at quilting. "My first quilt was huge, heavy, and appliquéd. The colors were hideous; the quilting stitches were gigantic. The materials I used were all wrong. Basically, I really had no idea what I was doing." It was such an overwhelming project, that it was several years before she attempted another. At the grocery store one day, she picked up a quilting magazine "just to look" and before she knew it, she was making quilts again.

When she got back into quilting, it was in a serious way. Her husband, Oliver, encouraged her to submit her quilts for publication and to try her hand at entering contests. Her first contest submission won a prize. Then she thought she'd try her hand at the 1997 Hoffman Challenge. To her amazement and delight, *Byzantine Compass* garnered a first place ribbon in the mixed technique category. Since then, Nancy's quilts have been featured in magazines such as *Quilter's Newsletter Magazine, McCalls Quilting, Quiltmaker,* and *Quilt.* Other quilts have appeared in calendars and books .

Oliver A. Rink has served as professor at California State University, Bakersfield, since 1975. As a member of the History Department, he has taught a wide variety of courses ranging from a bio-history course titled "Plagues and Peoples," co-taught with ecology Professor Maynard Moe, to a world history course series, to courses in American Colonial History, his area of expertise. He is the author of *Holland on the Hudson: An Economic and Social History of Dutch New York* that traces the history of New Netherland from Henry Hudson's exploration of the region in 1609 to the surrender of the Dutch colony to an English fleet in 1664. He is also a contributing author to *The Empire State: A History of New York.* After taking up cycling for about a year, Oliver rode in his first one-hundred mile race in 2011, finishing in the pouring rain.

Nancy and Oliver have three grown children: Diane, David, and Gary. They live in Bakersfield, California, with their dog Daisy.

ACKNOWLEDGMENTS

Many thanks go to the talented group of women at Marcus Fabrics. Working with Stephanie, Indra, Regina, Lisa and Brandy has been inspiring and a privilege. Thank you to Faye Burgos and Judie Rothermel for your design work on The Mill Girls fabric collection. You took an idea and created cloth beautiful to look at and to touch. And, special thanks go to Pati Violick for her mentorship and support.

Kudos to Donna di Natale for keeping everything on track for this book from start to finish, and for scouting out the perfect setting for photographing the quilts. Thanks to Kansas City Star Quilts for undertaking our big little project about the Lowell Mill Girls. Thank you to the talented team of Brian, Aaron, Jo Ann, Eric and Nan for their expertise in making this beautiful book.

Watkins Mill State Historic Site

The authors and Kansas City Star Quilts wish to extend their gratitude to Missouri State Parks, a division of the Missouri Department of Natural Resources, for allowing us to photograph the projects in this book at Watkins Woolen Mill State Park and State Historic Site.

The quilts in this book were all photographed on location in the Waltus Watkins home at Watkins Woolen Mill State Historic Site. Located in the rolling hills of Northwest Missouri, near the town of Kearney, Watkins Mill is the last fully equipped 19th century woolen mill in the United States. It has been designated as a National Historic Landmark and a National Mechanical Engineering Landmark.

While many mills still exist across the country, Watkins Mill is unique for the fact that it still retains its original equipment and layout, as seen on the pages in this book, and even shows the wear patterns left by the people who worked in the mill. In addition to the woolen mill and home, there is a school and a church on the grounds. The Visitor Center & Museum is the place to begin your exploration. Living History programs with costumed interpreters are held weekends during the summer.

Watkins Woolen Mill State Park and State Historic Site are managed by Missouri State Parks, a division of the Missouri Department of Natural Resources. For further information visit their web site at www.mostateparks.com.

Lowell Girls and America's First Industrial Revolution

The Factories

Between 1820 and 1860 the United States began the century-long transformation that would turn a nation of farmers and rural folk into a nation of workers living in towns and cities. The U.S. Census of 1820 indicated that 72% of the labor force worked on family farms. By 1860, the end of the first phase of industrialization, that number had dropped to 59%. In that same year, 41% of the nation's workers labored outside agriculture, and the process of urbanization was accelerating. During the same period the value of manufactured goods increased at a rate more than twice that of population growth. America was becoming an industrial giant among nations. (Thomas Dublin, *Women at Work: The Transformation of Work and Community in Lowell, Massachusetts, 1826-1860*, New York: Columbia University Press, 1979, p3.)

Moses Brown

America's industrial revolution began in New England's textile mills when Moses Brown, a wealthy Quaker merchant in Rhode Island, and Samuel Slater, a former apprentice and mechanic in English mills owned by Richard Arkwright, opened a textile factory in Pawtucket, Rhode Island. Slater had pulled off one of the greatest pieces of industrial espionage in history, having memorized intricate plans and diagrams of Arkwright's spinning and carding machines as well as long lists of specifications. The Brown-Slater Mill employed nine children between the ages of 7 and 12 and paid them 33 to 60 cents per week. Profits came quickly, and Slater and his partners poured them into more and bigger mills. Within a few years, Brown and Slater had become New England's leading industrialists with over a dozen mills in three states.

Samuel Slater

As New England textile mills grew larger and the machines bigger and faster, children began to suffer injuries. Public opinion eventually turned against the mill owners forcing them to seek another labor system. In Fall River, Massachusetts, mill owners tried a new system. Entire families were hired to work in the mills. The owners reasoned that with parental supervision children could be better managed. The system, however, failed to attract and hold men because wages were less than they could earn in agriculture, and factory work degraded the male head of the household by taking control of his wife and children. A factory hand could hardly object to a supervisor disciplining his wife or children. Consequently, New England men largely retreated to agriculture, but their wives and children flocked to the mills to supplement family income.

Francis Cabot Lowell, 1775-1817

The third great figure in the industrialization of textiles, Francis Cabot Lowell, was one of the most creative and innovative businessmen in American history. In 1813, having recently returned from a trip to Scotland and England, Lowell, a merchant, with the aid of Paul Moody, a mechanic, set out to build a power loom based on his memory of looms he had seen during his travels. With a working loom in hand, Lowell gathered several other Boston merchants together and petitioned a charter from the Massachusetts state legislature to build a cotton mill in Waltham. The merchants formed the Boston Manufacturing Company and set about obtaining start-up capital. The company developed a new means of raising capital by selling $1000 shares in the company — an investment of over $10,000 in 2011 dollars. This shareholder corporation, led by a board of hands-on directors, became the quintessential American model for capital formation and remains so to this day.

The factory at Waltham, Massachusetts, was something completely new to the industry. In the first instance it was larger than any mill yet constructed in America — ten times larger than the average Rhode Island mill at the time — and with an initial capital of $400,000 (over $10 million in 2011 dollars) it ranked as the largest industrial project ever undertaken in the United States. The Waltham factory was also the first fully integrated cotton mill in America, combining all the mechanization technologies to transform raw cotton into finished cloth under a single roof. Industrial integration allowed the Boston Manufacturing Company to enjoy enormous economies of scale, and almost immediately thrust Lowell and his partners into a dominant position in the textile industry. Mass production techniques allowed the Waltham factory to specialize in cheap, coarse goods for the mass market, opening up a domestic market as yet untapped by the Rhode Island firms that marketed yarns and hand-woven cloth for a relatively affluent urban population. (Dublin, *Women at Work*, p 17)

The Mill Girls

Arguably the Waltham factory's most interesting and socially significant innovation was the development of a female factory labor force. Scholars continue to debate the motivation behind this innovation. Certainly Waltham's remote location meant fewer children were available to work. Another consideration was the swifter pace of the machines that would have placed children at greater risk of injury and resulted in a public outcry against child labor. Whatever the motivation, the Boston Manufacturing Company decided to employ adult labor. The result was the so-called "Lowell System"— the first female industrial work force in history.

The system employed young, single women between 15 and 25 years of age drawn from the New England countryside. Farm girls mostly, they were lured from the protection of their families with promises of independence and good wages. Cautious New England fathers saw an opportunity to improve their daughters' marriage prospects through the building up of dowries, but pecuniary considerations were not the only concern. Factory agents had to work hard to recruit workers from skeptical and conservative parents by promising cultural and educational programs in the evenings, strict supervision of the girls' religious life, and a morally upright living environment. Women who did not reside with relatives were required to live in company boardinghouses, where regulations were clearly posted and all improper behavior immediately reported to mill managers.

REGULATIONS
FOR THE
BOARDING HOUSES
OF THE
MIDDLESEX COMPANY.

The tenants of the Boarding Houses are not to board, or permit any part of their houses to be occupied by any person except those in the employ of the Company.

They will be considered answerable for any improper conduct in their houses, and are not to permit their boarders to have company at unseasonable hours.

The doors must be closed at ten o'clock in the evening, and no one admitted after that time without some reasonable excuse.

The keepers of the Boarding Houses must give an account of the number, names, and employment of their boarders, when required; and report the names of such as are guilty of any improper conduct, or are not in the regular habit of attending public worship.

The buildings and yards about them must be kept clean and in good order, and if they are injured otherwise than from ordinary use, all necessary repairs will be made, and charged to the occupant.

It is indispensable that all persons in the employ of the Middlesex Company should be vaccinated who have not been, as also the families with whom they board; which will be done at the expense of the Company.

SAMUEL LAWRENCE, Agent.

JOEL TAYLOR, PRINTER, Daily Courier Office.

Boarding House Regulations

Boston Manufacturing Company,
Waltham Mill, 1813-1816

Most mills required that the girls attend Sunday worship at a church of their
choosing and prove it with a certificate signed by their minister. Some mills went
further. The Merrimack Company withheld the cost of pew rentals from the mill girls'
wages and paid the funds to the local Episcopal Church. Mill managers collaborated
with the boardinghouses to ensure a strict morality that included curfews, bed checks,
and opportunities for education and moral edification. This strict paternalism was in
keeping with the ethos of a rural society that feared the consequences of urban life and
sought to protect their daughters' reputations. It also served another purpose. The tightly
controlled, almost Puritanical, social system served to keep the recruits coming to the
factories.

Recruitment poster   Mill Girl

Mill Girls with bobbins

The successful experiment with a female labor force in Waltham served as the backdrop to the construction of Lowell, where the majority of mill operatives were drawn from the same cohort of farmer's daughters. Until the mid-1830s, the factories appear to have been benign places where young women could experience a world denied them on the farm. Parents trusted the companies to provide clean and safe working conditions for their daughters, and for the most part this trust was justified.

In her memoir, *Loom and Spindle, or Life Among the Early Mill Girls*, Harriet Hanson Robinson recalled the conditions she first encountered working as a child in a Lowell factory.

> *I do not recall any particular hardship connected with this life, except getting up so early in the morning, and to this habit I never was, and never shall be, reconciled, for it has taken nearly a lifetime for me to make up the sleep lost at that early age. But in every other respect it was a pleasant life. We were not hurried any more than was for our good, and no more work was required of us than we were able easily to do.*

(Harriet H. Robinson, *Loom and Spindle or Life Among the Early Mill Girls*, New York: Thomas Y. Crowell & Company, 1898, pp 31-32.)

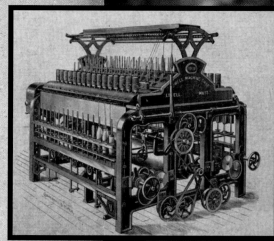

Spinning Frame

Certainly by modern standards the hours were long and the work tedious. The longest hours were in the summer months, when the women had to operate their machines for 14 hours. They were given brief breaks for breakfast and dinner, but these tended to be hurried affairs that ended with the ringing of the bell calling the women back to work. The winter schedule was shorter, but even then they spent the first and last hours of each day in the flickering light of oil lamps. In letters home to their families and in their diaries the young women complained of the bells that came to dominate their daily life.

In the summer, the first bells rang at 4:30 a.m. calling them to the factory; a second bell at 4:50 called them back to the boardinghouses to breakfast. Bells continued throughout the workday, calling them to lunch and dinner and finally sending them home at 7 p.m. By agreement all the mills set their bells to the same schedule.

Timetable of the Lowell Mills

A fictional character in a short story that appeared in the Lowell Offering in 1841 expressed what might have been the view of many.

> I object to the constant hurry of every thing. We cannot have time to eat, drink or sleep; we have only thirty minutes, or at most three quarters of an hour, allowed us, to go from our work, partake of our food, and return to the noisy clatter of machinery. Up before day, at the clang of the bell–and out of the mill by the clang of the bell–into the mill, and at work, in obedience to that ding-dong of a bell–just as though we were so many living machines.

(Benita Eisler, ed., *The Lowell Offering: Writings by New England Mill Women, 1840-1845*, New York: W.W. Norton & Company, 1998, p 161.)

The dissatisfaction expressed above may have been a response to a worsening of working conditions that began in the 1830s. In February 1834, the Board of Directors of Lowell's textile mills agreed to reduce wages by 15%, effective March 1. The decision came out of a protracted discussion involving all the mills' directors. The directors justified the wage cut on the basis of falling prices of textiles goods, a sluggish domestic market and rising inventories of unsold cloth. At the initial meeting the directors agreed to a 25% wage cut, but company agents responsible for the recruitment of workers attempted to mitigate the cuts. The agents' efforts seemed to have had some effect because, at a subsequent meeting, the directors and agents agreed on a 15% wage cut. (Dublin, *Women at Work*, p 90.)

The mill girls hastily organized meetings and signed petitions to protest the wage reduction. One petition, signed by 50 weavers at the Suffolk Company threatened a strike if the reduction went into effect. The Suffolk Company petitioners sent their petition to weavers at the Appleton Company, calling on them to take up the cause. During the dinner breaks women held meetings and were slow to return to their stations. Managers reported that work was being disrupted by the agitation. One manager made the mistake of firing a woman he considered a leader. Immediately her fellow workers shut down production and walked off the job. They marched through the streets of Lowell stopping at each mill to persuade others to join.

In all about 800 women joined in the procession, roughly one-sixth of all women workers in Lowell at the time. The marchers assembled at a mass rally in the center of Lowell, where, according to the Boston *Evening Transcript*, one of the leaders made a speech "on the rights of women and the iniquities of the *monied* aristocracy," which met with rousing cheers and inspired the strikers "to have their own way if they died for it." (Dublin, *Women at Work*, p 91.) The strikers also withdrew their savings in Lowell banks, causing a run on two of the banks. The strike, however, failed to attract enough workers to shut down production completely, and within days the women returned to their machines at the reduced wage. Others quit and left town rather than face being blacklisted. Nonetheless, the strike aroused much sympathy among the Nation's rising labor movements and demonstrated the determination of the mill girls to protest and organize.

Fabric collection

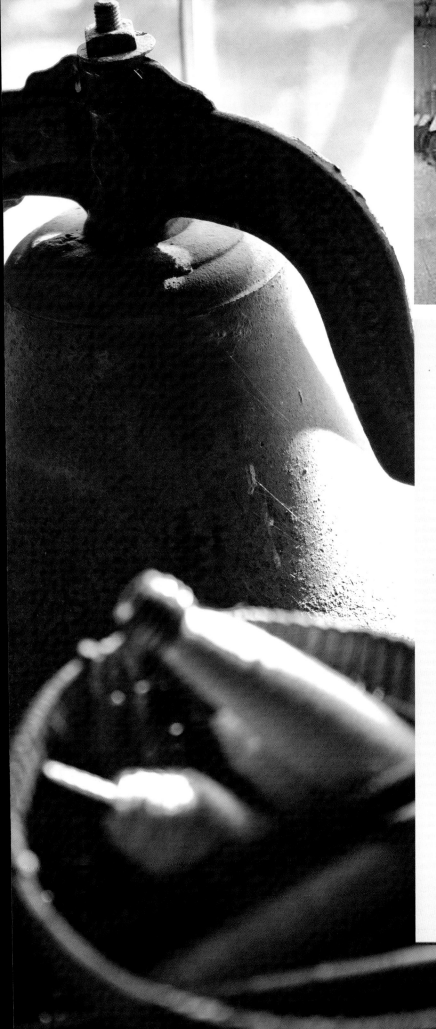

NATIONAL THEATRE.

Grand Gala Performance.   Immense Success of the NEW DRAMA.

Revival of JACK SHEPPARD! Jack Sheppard, Miss Mestayer, as played by her with unbounded applause at the New York and Philadelphia Theatres.

Doors open at 1-4 before 7 o'clock, and the performance will commence at 1-4 past 7.

Thursday Evening, Sept. 20th, 1849,

Will be performed (9th time) the exciting Drama, in 4 acts, written for this Theatre by W. B. English, the popular author of the highly successful Dramas of Boston Boys and Boston Girls, Mike Martin, &c., entitled the

MILL GIRLS OF LOWELL

OR, LIGHTS AND SHADOWS OF FACTORY LIFE!

WITH

Mysteries of Lowell, Dover, Nashua, and Manchester.

A DRAMA OF INNOCENCE AND GUILT.

The Scenery painted from Original sketches by Mr Hayes.   The Mechanical Effects by Mr Gill. Properties by Mr J. Stories. Costumes by Mrs Dwinell. The Music by Mr Mayer. Dances by Mr Pierce.

Act I—ROMANCE AND RASCALITY.

ABODE OF A BOSTON MAN OF FASHION.   A traveller at the Court of St James, and the Fashionable Spas in the U. S.   The Belle of Lowell.   Hearts are trumps.   Puss in a corner.   Opening of a nigger's eye balls.   Beware of a cat's claws.   Georgiana discovers an error in her affianced bridegroom.   A maid n's stratagem.   "You may conquer old nick, but you can't deceive a woman."

View of the Lowell Depot, foot of Lowell Street, Boston, with Bunker Hill Monument and Charlestown in the distance.

Starting of the Train.   A miss is as good as a mile.   'If you don't wish to be left, you must come up to the time.'   An unpleasant incident that has happened to many.   Yankee curiosity.   The Pump and sucker dry.   Arrival in Lowell.   **Railroad Depot in Middlesex Street.**   The Train in. Attempted Robbery.   Foul Play.   Manly conduct.   Lights of Factory Life.

Act 2d. LIGHTS OF FACTORY LIFE!

VIEW OF LOWELL.   The Yankee and his paint pot.   Mark him well.   The Boston Belle disguised as the Lowell Buck.   Oysters raised in Boston and fatted up in Lowell.   Two Green 'Uns.   The home of a scoundrel.   The Plot thickens.   Two Professors of Vice.   MARSTON'S FASHIONABLE RESTAURANT.   "Oysters for individuals and parties.   Corned Beef, Fish and Clam Chowders."   The bloods of Lowell on a spree.   A quarrel.   Pistols for two.   The Nabob's return from Calcutta.   The Great City of Spindl s.   The Nabob and the Italian in his own character. Room in the Middlesex Mills.   The Machines.   Operatives   Diabolical Plot.

'Did you ever go into Lowell, Oh! rackett, | Like fifty five crabs in a buck t,
Good Lord what a buzzing it makes, | And what a darned sight of cotton it takes.'

Factory Boarding House; terms 1.25 a week and not found.   Mrs Bustle no friend to large corporations.   An intrigue.   Two distinguished Foreigners in the field.   Humors of the Factory Girls.   Shower Baths in operation.   Laughable Tableaus.

Act 3...SHADOWS OF FACTORY LIFE!

Farmer's Home; the Wicked and the Good; a Villain Foiled; oppressive measures of Old Roper;

For the male mill directors, managers, and agents the response was one of shock and surprise. For them the strike was unfeminine, a betrayal of the idealized image of women. The charge of being unfeminine would follow all efforts by women to obtain civil rights for the next century, but in the 1830s the allegation was still new, and it was felt deeply by the women who suffered it. When women operatives established the first quasi-union, the Lowell Factory Girls' Association in 1836, they were careful in the preamble to the Association's constitution, to couch their aims within the cultural milieu of the day. Having established their "love of honest industry and the expectation of a fair and liberal recompense" for their work, they reassured the public that their demands were in keeping with "a modesty becoming our sex." They went on to announce their intention and duty "to incite each other to the love and attainment of those excellences, which can alone constitute the perfection of female character – unsullied virtue, refined tastes, and cultivated intellects – and in a word, do all that in us lies, to make each other worthy ourselves, our country, and Creator." Having reassured a critical public of their femininity in the preamble, they included as Article 12 a provision to expel any member from the Association whose conduct was deemed immoral, or whose behavior was "unbecoming respectable and virtuous females." In Article 10 they threatened economic boycotts of merchants and banks that opposed their right to organize, stating that "it shall forever be the policy of the members of this Association, to bestow their patronage, so far as is practicable, upon such persons as befriend, but never upon such as oppose our cause."

The founding of the Lowell Factory Girls' Association was prompted by yet another attack on their livelihoods. In October 1836, in response to company boardinghouse keepers' complaints that they could no longer make ends meet due to rapid inflation, the Lowell mill directors decided to raise the price of room and board. This action sparked a flurry of activity as rumors of the impending price increase swept through the mills. By placing all of the increased costs of housing and board on the workers,

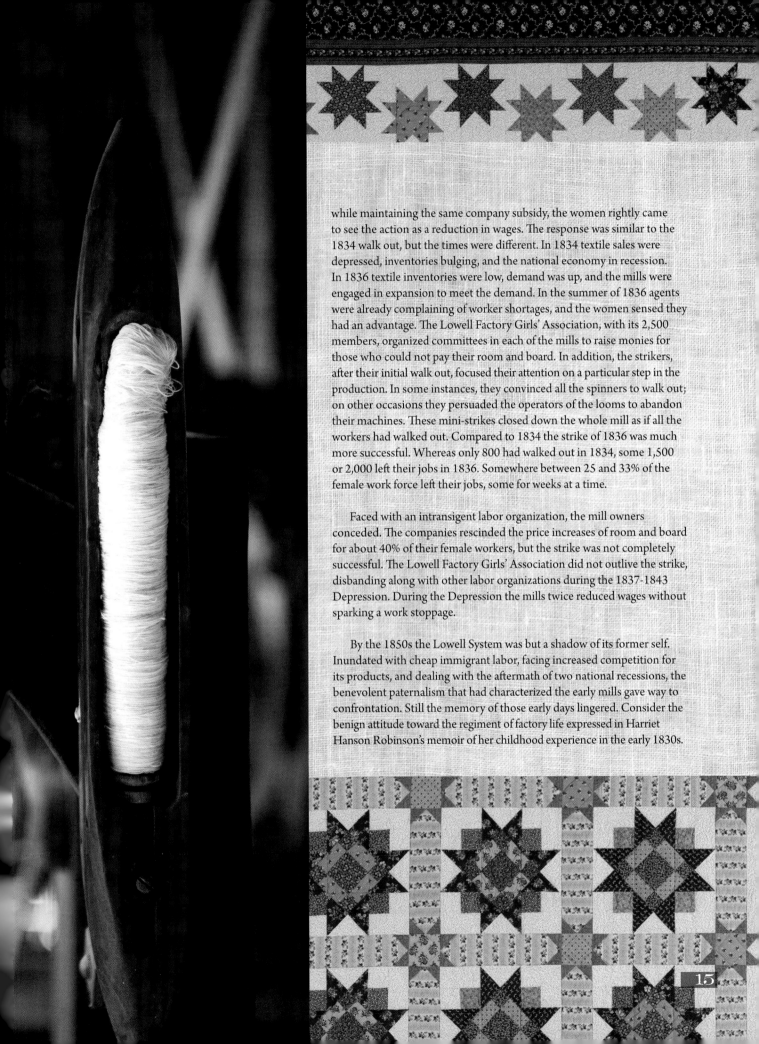

while maintaining the same company subsidy, the women rightly came to see the action as a reduction in wages. The response was similar to the 1834 walk out, but the times were different. In 1834 textile sales were depressed, inventories bulging, and the national economy in recession. In 1836 textile inventories were low, demand was up, and the mills were engaged in expansion to meet the demand. In the summer of 1836 agents were already complaining of worker shortages, and the women sensed they had an advantage. The Lowell Factory Girls' Association, with its 2,500 members, organized committees in each of the mills to raise monies for those who could not pay their room and board. In addition, the strikers, after their initial walk out, focused their attention on a particular step in the production. In some instances, they convinced all the spinners to walk out; on other occasions they persuaded the operators of the looms to abandon their machines. These mini-strikes closed down the whole mill as if all the workers had walked out. Compared to 1834 the strike of 1836 was much more successful. Whereas only 800 had walked out in 1834, some 1,500 or 2,000 left their jobs in 1836. Somewhere between 25 and 33% of the female work force left their jobs, some for weeks at a time.

Faced with an intransigent labor organization, the mill owners conceded. The companies rescinded the price increases of room and board for about 40% of their female workers, but the strike was not completely successful. The Lowell Factory Girls' Association did not outlive the strike, disbanding along with other labor organizations during the 1837-1843 Depression. During the Depression the mills twice reduced wages without sparking a work stoppage.

By the 1850s the Lowell System was but a shadow of its former self. Inundated with cheap immigrant labor, facing increased competition for its products, and dealing with the aftermath of two national recessions, the benevolent paternalism that had characterized the early mills gave way to confrontation. Still the memory of those early days lingered. Consider the benign attitude toward the regiment of factory life expressed in Harriet Hanson Robinson's memoir of her childhood experience in the early 1830s.

The discipline our work brought us was of great value. We were obliged to be in the mill at just such a minute, in every hour, in order to doff our full bobbins and replace them with empty ones. We went to our meals and returned at the same hour every day. We worked and played at regular intervals, and thus our hands became deft, our fingers nimble, our feet swift, and were taught daily habits of regularity and of industry; it was, in fact, a sort of manual training or industrial school. (Robinson, *Loom and Spindle*, p 42)

Compared to other occupations available to women at the time, millwork offered a number of advantages, especially in the 1820s and early 1830s. Unlike the older mills in New England that paid workers with credit at the company store, the Boston Associates early on established monthly payment of cash wages. During the 1830s a woman might earn $12 to $14 monthly. Even after deducting $5 for lodging and meals at a company boardinghouse, she could pocket more money than she could ever have working on a farm, serving as a teacher, or doing domestic service. It was not uncommon for young women to return home after a year with $25 to $50 dollars in a bank account. Mill girls had money to buy clothes, put away for a dowry, and assist their parents. Such financial independence had never been available to women before, and it had a transformative effect.

The discretionary income of the mill girls also had a transformative effect on the town of Lowell. In 1848 over half of the depositors in the Lowell Institution for Savings were mill employees and over one-third of the deposits belonged to women workers, a sum of over $100,000 or roughly $1,000,000 in 2011 dollars. (Robinson, *Loom and Spindle*, p 18.) Certainly some of this money was destined for a future dowry or to support aged parents, but it appears clear that many of the mill girls' families assumed the wages were the girls' to spend.

For some of these young women life in the factory town became the adventure of their lives — the equivalent of going away to college. They worked long hours, to be sure, but they also checked out books from one of Lowell's circulating libraries, attended factory-sponsored seminars, heard recitals by some of the finest musicians of the day, and took in lectures at the Lowell Lyceum. During the winter season, Lyceum lectures, alternating with concerts, covered the hottest topics of the day both literary and scientific. All the stars of the Lyceum circuit made an appearance in Lowell: John Quincy Adams, Edward Everett, Horace Mann, Horace Greeley, and Ralph Waldo Emerson. In the winter of 1839 one could have heard Emerson speak on "Ethical English Literature," attended a lecture on "The Use of Wine," and heard a presentation on "Palestine and Egypt." By the early 1840s seven Mutual Self-Improvement Clubs had been established in Lowell, where members could meet to read their essays and short stories, or find an audience for their poetry.

17

In the 1840s at the suggestion of a minister in Lowell, Harriet F. Curtis and Harriet Farley founded the literary magazine, *The Lowell Offering*. In its five-year run, from 1840 to 1845, it published dozens of pieces written by mill women. The articles ran the gamut from nostalgic reminiscences of small town Christmases to political diatribes in defense of mill girls' reputations. The *Offering* came to represent the counter argument to the accusations of traditionalists who claimed that factory work attracted women of doubtful moral character. The intended audience was the urban middle class, whose prejudice against the mill girls had appeared frequently in Boston newspaper editorials. The idea of single young women living apart from their families in company boardinghouses conjured up a host of fears of promiscuity, masculinity, and the break up of the family. To middle class inhabitants of Boston the mill girls became just another example of the collapse of family values and the debasement of the female ideal. The editors of the *Offering* made a conscious decision to avoid controversial issues and generally stayed clear of the debate on wages and working conditions that came to dominate the concerns of the mill girls in the late 1840s. They opposed the Ten Hour Movement and for the most part remained silent when the mill owners engaged in efforts to speed up the machines, reduce wages, and raise boardinghouse fees.

FARLEY, HARRIET,

In 1847 the former editor of the *Lowell Offering*, Harriet Farley, revived the magazine under the new title of *The New England Offering*. In her introduction to the first issue Farley revealed the motives behind its predecessor's publication.

> *The Lowell Offering was established to prove that goodness and intelligence could and did exist in a factory community, and to remove the prejudice which had affixed itself to the cognomen of 'Factory Girl.'* (Harriet Farley, *The New England Offering*, Vol.1, Sep. 1847)

By 1850 the native-born labor force had been replaced by a majority of Irish immigrants. The arrival of immigrants brought an end to the Lowell experiment. The benign paternalism of the early days had become a faint memory.

Cover of *The Lowell Offering* from October 1845

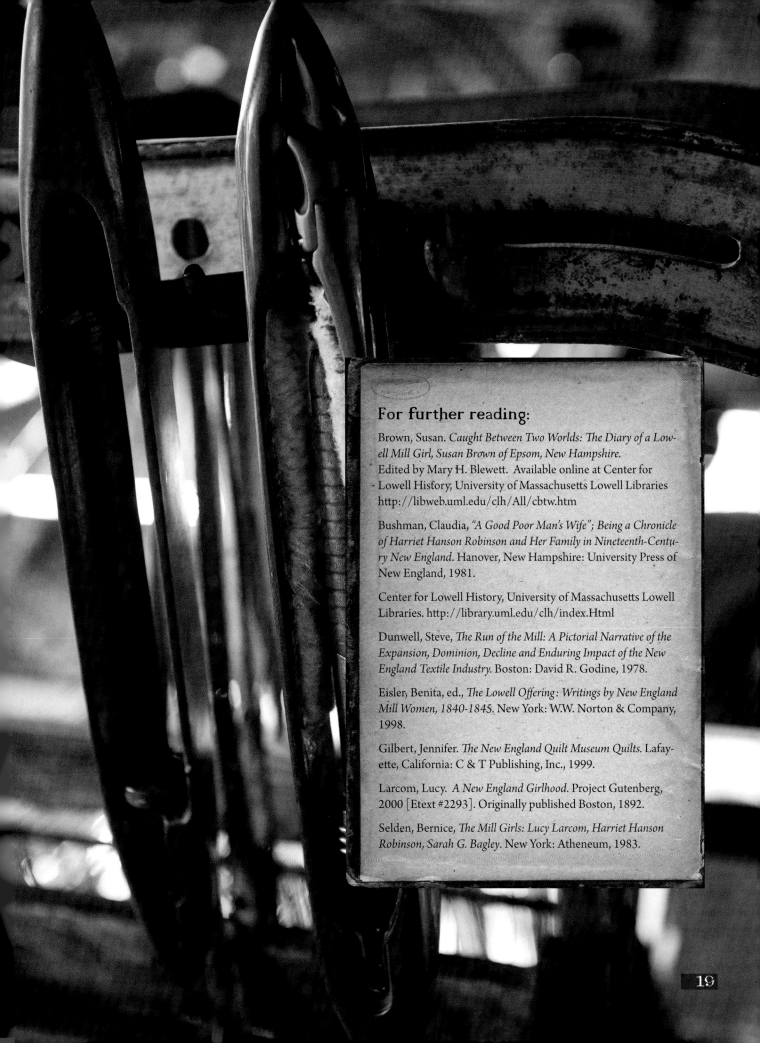

For further reading:

Brown, Susan. *Caught Between Two Worlds: The Diary of a Lowell Mill Girl, Susan Brown of Epsom, New Hampshire.* Edited by Mary H. Blewett. Available online at Center for Lowell History, University of Massachusetts Lowell Libraries http://libweb.uml.edu/clh/All/cbtw.htm

Bushman, Claudia, *"A Good Poor Man's Wife"; Being a Chronicle of Harriet Hanson Robinson and Her Family in Nineteenth-Century New England.* Hanover, New Hampshire: University Press of New England, 1981.

Center for Lowell History, University of Massachusetts Lowell Libraries. http://library.uml.edu/clh/index.Html

Dunwell, Steve, *The Run of the Mill: A Pictorial Narrative of the Expansion, Dominion, Decline and Enduring Impact of the New England Textile Industry.* Boston: David R. Godine, 1978.

Eisler, Benita, ed., *The Lowell Offering: Writings by New England Mill Women, 1840-1845.* New York: W.W. Norton & Company, 1998.

Gilbert, Jennifer. *The New England Quilt Museum Quilts.* Lafayette, California: C & T Publishing, Inc., 1999.

Larcom, Lucy. *A New England Girlhood.* Project Gutenberg, 2000 [Etext #2293]. Originally published Boston, 1892.

Selden, Bernice, *The Mill Girls: Lucy Larcom, Harriet Hanson Robinson, Sarah G. Bagley.* New York: Atheneum, 1983.

The Fabrics

The fabrics used in this book were all designed by Judie Rothermel for Marcus Fabrics. *The Mill Girls 1830 - 1850* collection was designed especially for the projects in this book. Working with the curator of Old Sturbridge Village in Massachusetts, Judie carefully selected fabric patterns indicative of the era in which the Lowell Mill Girls lived.

THE MILL GIRLS 1830-1850 fabric collection

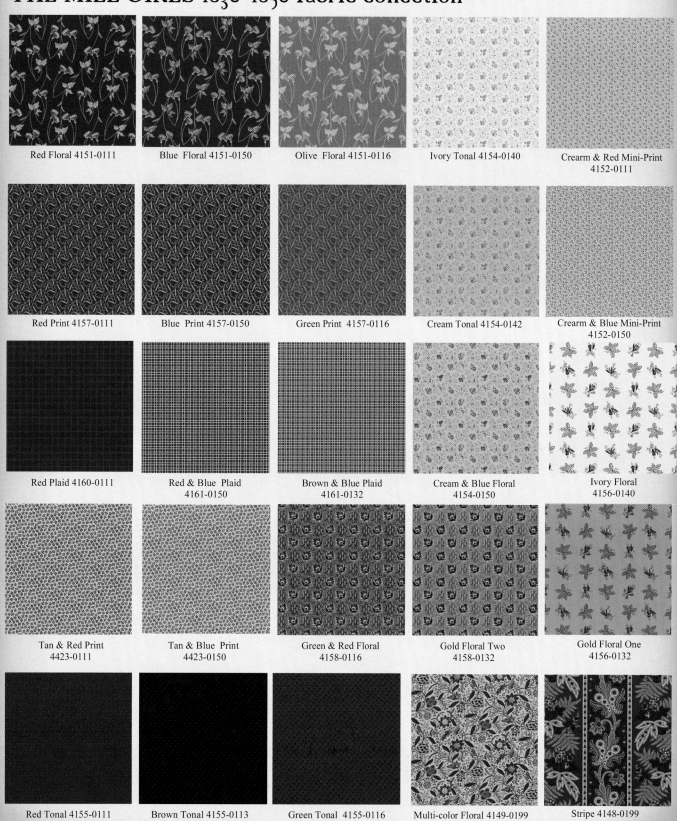

Red Floral 4151-0111

Blue Floral 4151-0150

Olive Floral 4151-0116

Ivory Tonal 4154-0140

Crearm & Red Mini-Print
4152-0111

Red Print 4157-0111

Blue Print 4157-0150

Green Print 4157-0116

Cream Tonal 4154-0142

Crearm & Blue Mini-Print
4152-0150

Red Plaid 4160-0111

Red & Blue Plaid
4161-0150

Brown & Blue Plaid
4161-0132

Cream & Blue Floral
4154-0150

Ivory Floral
4156-0140

Tan & Red Print
4423-0111

Tan & Blue Print
4423-0150

Green & Red Floral
4158-0116

Gold Floral Two
4158-0132

Gold Floral One
4156-0132

Red Tonal 4155-0111

Brown Tonal 4155-0113

Green Tonal 4155-0116

Multi-color Floral 4149-0199

Stripe 4148-0199

FABRIC REQUIREMENTS

Yardage given here is for the entire quilt. Please refer to the fabric swatches (p. 21) as you pick the fabrics for the quilt blocks. Templates for the blocks can be found on pages 81-94 and are referred to in the instructions by their alphabet letter.

Away From Home

Blue Floral 4151-0150 – 5/8 yard
Blue Print 4157-0150 – 5/8 yard
Brown & Blue Plaid 4161-0132 – 1/2 yard
Brown Tonal 4155-0113 – 2 yards
Cream & Blue Floral 4154-0150 – 3/8 yard
Cream & Blue Mini-print 4152-0150 – 1/2 yard
Cream & Red Mini-print 4152-0111 – 1 5/8 yard
Cream Tonal 4154-0142 – 1/4 yard

Gold Floral One 4156-0132 – 3/4 yard
Gold Floral Two 4158-0132 – 1/2 yard
Green & Red Floral 4158-0116 – 1/2 yard
Green Print 4157-0116 – 1/2 yard
Green Tonal 4155-0116 – 3/4 yard
Ivory Floral 4156-0140 – 3/4 yard
Ivory Tonal 4154-0140 – 2 1/2 yards
Multi-color Floral 4149-0199 – 3/4 yard
Olive Floral 4151-0116 – 3/8 yard
Red & Blue Plaid 4161-0150 – 3/8 yard

Red Floral 4151-0111 – 1/2 yard
Red Plaid 4160-0111 – 1/2 yard
Red Print 4157-0111 – 1/4 yard
Red Tonal 4155-0111 2 1/4 yard
Stripe 4148-0199 – 2 1/2 yards
Tan & Blue Print 4423-0150 – 5/8 yard
Tan & Red Print 4423-0111 – 5/8 yard
108"-wide Backing Fabric 4420 - 0122 (multi-color) or 4420 - 0166 (tan/tan) – 3 1/8 yards

The Mill Girls

FINISHED SIZE: 20" x 20"

MAKE 1 BLOCK

FABRIC REQUIREMENTS

Ivory Tonal 4154-0140 for background
Green Print 4157-0116 for grass
Tan & Blue Print 4423-0150 for windows
Red Plaid 4160-0111 for factory and chimneys
Brown & Blue Plaid 4161-0132 for factory roof
Gold Floral One 4156-0132 for sun
Gold Floral Two 4158-0132 for moon
Brown Tonal 4155-0113 for shoes, hair, and bobbins
Cream Tonal 4154-0142 for face, neck, and hands
Red & Blue Plaid 4161-0150 for blouses
Blue Floral 4151-0150 for skirt
Ivory Floral 4156-0140 for aprons
Blue Print 4157-0150 for skirt

SEWING INSTRUCTIONS

1. Fold and crease the Ivory Tonal square vertically to create a placement guide line for appliqué.

2. Using the reverse appliqué method of your choice, sew the Factory B to the Tan & Blue print rectangle. Trim away excess Tan & Blue print fabric.

3. Position the Factory, 2 Chimneys, and the Roof on the background fabric, aligning vertical centers of the Roof and the Factory with the vertical center of the block. Pin or glue appliqué pieces in place. Appliqué using matching thread.

4. Refer to the *Block Placement Diagram* on page 81 to position and secure the remaining appliqué pieces. Using your method of choice, appliqué pieces to the background using matching thread.

5. On the Mill Girl figures, some of the appliqué pieces are tucked under others (i.e., hands and skirts). This requires you to leave some areas unsewn until you can tuck these pieces under, before you complete the appliqué.

2. Press block from the wrong side and trim to 20 1/2" x 20 1/2".

CUTTING DIRECTIONS

Use templates on page (s) 81-86.

From the Ivory Tonal, cut: 1 – 21"square
From the Green Print, cut: 1 – A
From the Tan & Blue Print, cut:1 – 8 1/4" x 12" rectangle
From the Red Plaid, cut: 1 – B; 2 – C; 1 – Y
From the Brown & Blue Plaid, cut: 1 – D
From the Gold Floral One cut: 1 – E; 12 – F
From the Gold Floral Two, cut: 1 – G
From the Brown Tonal, cut: 1 each – H, I, K, M, N, T, V, W, X, BB, CC, FF
From the Cream Tonal, cut: 1 each – J, L, S, U, Z, AA, GG
From the Red & Blue Plaid, cut: 1 each – O, HH
From the Blue Floral, cut: 1 – P
From the Ivory Floral, cut: 1 each – Q, R, EE, II
From the Blue Print, cut: 1 – DD

FARLEY, HARRIET,

Harriet Farley

Harriet Farley was born in Claremont, New Hampshire in 1813 (some sources claim 1817) to a large family headed by the Reverend Stephen Farley. Poor and barely able to support his large brood of ten children, Reverend Farley came to depend on his older children to find work. As the sixth of ten children, young Harriet took a number of menial jobs and taught school. At the age of twenty-five she decided against a career as a teacher and, against the wishes of her family, moved to Lowell. There she quickly acquired a position in the mills. Her education and maturity contrasted sharply with many of her co-workers, and she was eager to take advantage of the many lectures and cultural improvement opportunities provided by the Lowell System. From a very early age she developed a moral objection to slavery, and in Lowell she found the opportunity to throw herself into the antislavery crusade. Although she worked 12 hours a day, six days a week, she found time to pen a long reply to the famed transcendentalist Orestes Brownson, who had written that the work in the mills "was far more oppressed than slave labor…" Her spirited defense of the mill girls as virtuous and hardworking was published in the *Lowell Offering* in 1840. Two years later Harriet, with her friend Harriot Curtis, departed the mills to co-edit the *Lowell Offering*. The next year she joined the Massachusetts Anti-Slavery Society, formed by William Lloyd Garrison to advocate the abolition of slavery. She became one of the nation's strongest female voices against the continuation of the "peculiar institution." In Lowell she helped organize fundraisers, organize gatherings and sponsor speeches on behalf of the abolitionist movement.

By the mid-1840s the Lowell experiment was fraying as the mill owners pushed to lower wages, raise boarding house fees, and speed up the machines. In 1845 Harriet suffered criticism from her former friend Sarah G. Bagley for her refusal to address the issues of the day in the pages of the *Lowell Offering*. Bagley accused her of serving as "the mouthpiece for the corporation." The criticism stung Farley, and the magazine's reputation suffered. The *Lowell Offering* ceased publication that same year. Two years later Farley tried to revive the magazine under a new name, the *New England Offering*, that accepted submissions from working women throughout New England. Several of the pieces published in the new magazine dealt with the issues of labor reform, but it too succumbed to a shrinking readership and ceased publication altogether in 1850. Shortly thereafter Farley moved to New York City, where she contributed a number of articles to *Godey's Lady's Book*. In 1851 she published a collection of her father's essays, entitled *Discourses and Essays on Theological and Speculative Topics*. In 1853 she published a children's book, *Happy Nights at Hazel Nook*.

The following year she married an engraver and inventor John Dunlevy. He disapproved of her writing career, and she put down her pen for the next thirty-six years to raise a family. Following her husband's death she published her last work, a Christmas book, *Fancy's Frolics*, in 1880. She died in New York City on November 12, 1907.

The Blue Birds

FINISHED SIZE: 20" x 12"

MAKE 1 BLOCK

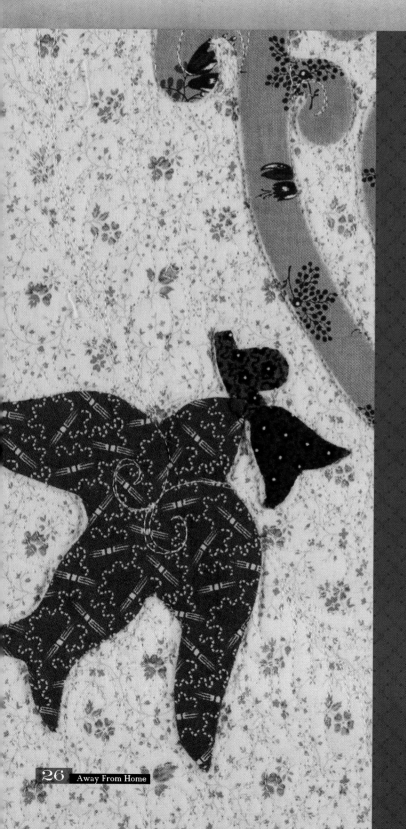

FABRIC REQUIREMENTS

Ivory Tonal 4154-0140 for background
Gold Floral One 4156-0132 for scrolled heart
Red Floral 4151-0111 for heart
Green Tonal 4155-0116 for stem and leaf
Red Tonal 4155-0111 for tulips
Blue Print 4157-0150 for birds

CUTTING DIRECTIONS

Use templates on page(s) 87-90.

From the Ivory Tonal, cut: 1 – 21" x 13" rectangle
From the Gold Floral One, cut: 1 – A
From the Red Floral, cut: 1 – B
From the Green Tonal, cut: 1 each – C and Cr
From the Blue Print, cut: 1each – E and Er
From the Red Tonal, cut: 1 each D and Dr

SEWING INSTRUCTIONS

1. Refer to the *Block Placement Diagram* on page 87 to position and secure appliqué pieces. Using your method of choice, appliqué pieces to the background.

2. Press block from the wrong side and trim to 20 1/2" x 12 1/2".

Lowell Nov 5th 1848

Dear Father

Doubtless you have been looking for a letter from me all the week past. I would have written but wished to find whether I should be able to stand it—to do the work that I am now doing. I was unable to get my old place in the cloth room on the Suffolk or on any other corporation. I next tried the dressrooms on the Lawrence Cor, but did not succeed in getting a place. I almost concluded to give up and go back to Claremont, but thought I would try once more. So I went to my old overseer on the Tremont Cor. I had no idea that he would want one, but he did, and I went to work last Tuesday warping—the same work I used to do.

It is very hard indeed and sometimes I think I shall not be able to endure it. I never worked so hard in my life but perhaps I shall get used to it. I shall try hard to do so for there is no other work that I can do unless I spin and that I shall not undertake on any account. I presume you have heard before this that the wages are to be reduced on the 20th of this month. It is true and there seems to be a good deal of excitement on the subject but I can not tell what will be the consequence. The companies pretend they are losing immense sums every day and therefore they are obliged to lessen the wages, but this seems perfectly absurd to me for they are constantly making repairs and it seems to me that this would not be if there were really any danger of their being obliged to stop the mills.

It is very difficult for any one to get into the mill on any corporation. All seem to be very full of help. I expect to be paid about two dollars a week but it will be dearly earned. I cannot tell how it is but never since I have worked in the mill have I been so very tired as I have for the last week …

Yours affectionately,
Mary S. Paul

From the Vermont Historical Society

The Trees

FINISHED SIZE: 10" X 32" BLOCKS

MAKE 2 BLOCKS

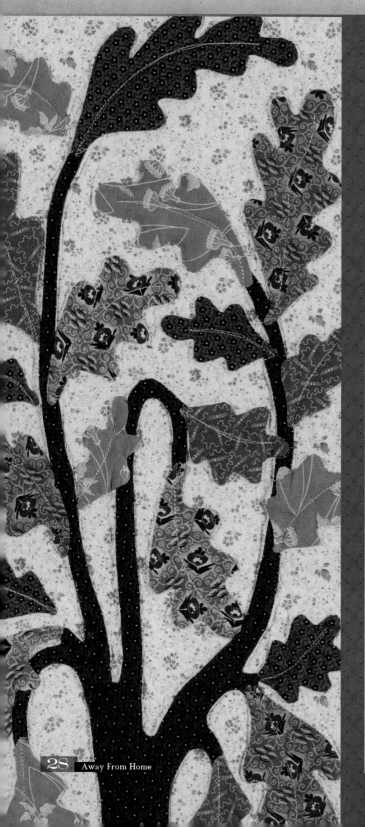

FABRIC REQUIREMENTS

Ivory Tonal 4154-0140 for background
Brown Tonal 4155-0113 for tree trunk
Green Print 4157-0116 for grass and leaves
Green & Red Floral 4158-0116 for leaves
Olive Floral 4151-0116 for leaves
Green Tonal 4155-0116 for leaves
Gold Floral Two 4158-0132 for leaves

CUTTING DIRECTIONS

Use templates on pages 91-94. Please note that you will be making 2 tree blocks, 1 a reverse of the other. The cutting instructions listed below are for both blocks.

From the Ivory Tonal, cut: 2 – 11" x 33" rectangles
From the Brown Tonal, cut: 1 each B and Br
From the Green Print, cut: 2 – A; 2 each G and Gr;
   1 each C and Cr; 1 each D and Dr
From the Green & Red Floral, cut: 1 each E and Er;
   1 each F and Fr; 1each G and Gr
From the Olive Floral, cut: 1 each C and Cr; 2 each D and Dr;
   1 each E and Er; 1 each G and Gr
From the Green Tonal, cut: 4 each C and Cr;
   1 each D and Dr; 1 each F and Fr
From the Gold Floral Two, cut: 3 each E and Er

SEWING INSTRUCTIONS

1. Refer to the *Tree Block Placement Diagram* on page 94 to position and secure appliqué pieces. Using your method of choice, appliqué pieces to the background.

2. Press the block from the wrong side and trim to 10 1/2" x 32 1/2".

29

Spool Blocks

FINISHED SIZE: 4" x 4" BLOCKS

MAKE 20 BLOCKS

FABRIC REQUIREMENTS

Backgrounds:
> Cream & Blue Floral 4154-0150
> Cream & Blue Mini-Print 4152-0150
> Cream & Red Mini-Print 4152-0111
> Tan & Red Print 4423-0111

Spools:
> Gold Floral Two 4158-0132
> Blue Print 4157-0150
> Brown & Blue Plaid 4161-0132
> Red & Blue Plaid 4161-0150

Thread:
> Red & Blue Plaid 4161-0150
> Gold Floral One 4156-0132
> Blue Floral 4151-0150
> Red Print 4157-0111

CUTTING DIRECTIONS

From each of the Background fabrics, cut: 30 – 1 7/8" A squares

From each of the Spool fabrics, cut: 10 – 1 7/8" x 4 1/2" B rectangles

From each of the Thread fabrics, cut: 5 – 1 7/8" A squares

SEWING INSTRUCTIONS

Below are the fabric combinations used in the quilt to make the Spool blocks.
Make 5 spool blocks from each of the fabric combinations.

Cream & Blue Floral / Gold Floral Two / Red & Blue Plaid
Cream & Blue Mini-Print / Blue Print / Gold Floral One
Cream & Red Mini-Print / Brown & Blue Plaid / Blue Floral
Tan & Red Print / Red & Blue Plaid / Red Print

1. To make one block you need 2 matching rectangles from Spool fabric, 6 matching A squares from Background fabric, and 1 A square from Thread fabric.

2. Sew together 2 Background A squares and 1 Thread A square as shown in *Diagram 1*. Press seams toward center.

Diagram 1

3. Lay a Background A square on top of the left-hand side of a Spool B rectangle, right sides together *(Diagram 2)*. On the wrong side of the Background A, draw a line diagonally from corner to corner. Sew on the line. Trim seam allowances to 1/4", flip open, and press. Next, place a Background A square on top to the right-hand side of the Spool B rectangle, right sides together. Draw a seam line diagonally from corner to corner. Sew on the line. Trim seam allowance to 1/4", flip open, and press. Make a total of two matching units.

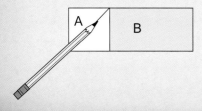 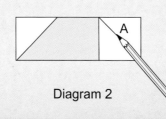 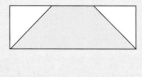

Diagram 2

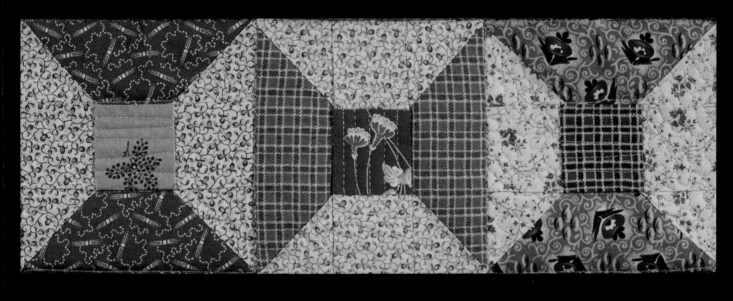

4. Lay out units and sew together, matching seams (*Diagram 3*). Make a total of 20 Spool Blocks.

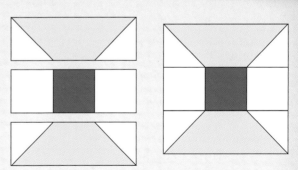

5. To make the Spool block rows, lay out 10 blocks, rotating alternate blocks as shown in *Diagram 4*. Sew together. Make two rows.

Diagram 3

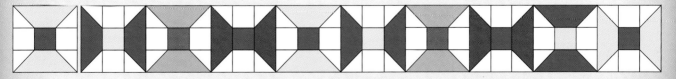

Diagram 4
Make 2 rows

Lucy Larcom, Poet Laureate of the Mill Girls

Lucy Larcom was born in Beverly, Massachusetts, in 1824, the second youngest of ten children. A precocious child, she learned to read at an early age under the supervision of her aunt, a schoolteacher. She attended private school with her sisters until age eleven, when the death of her father plunged the Larcom family into destitution. The family then moved to Lowell where her mother took up the duties of managing a boarding house belonging to the Lawrence Mills. Still strapped for cash, Lucy and her siblings entered the mill as children. Her first job was as a doffer. She was able to attend school three months of the year. By the age of thirteen she was ready to matriculate to high school, but her family's financial circumstances required her to work the mill fulltime instead. She became a spinner, working twelve hours shifts, six days a week, for a wage of $1.75 a week. Always the dreamer and poet, she found the work tedious and the machinery noisy and intimidating.

The noise of machinery was particularly distasteful to me. But I found that the crowd was made up of single human lives, not one of them wholly uninteresting, when separately known. I learned also that there are many things which belong to the whole world of us together, that no one of us, nor any few of us, can claim or enjoy for ourselves alone. I discovered, too, that I could so accustom myself to the noise that it became like a silence to me. And I defied the machinery to make me its slave. Its incessant discords could not drown the music of my thoughts if I would let them fly high enough. Even the long hours, the early rising and the regularity enforced by the clangor of the bell were good discipline for one who was naturally inclined to dally and to dream, and who loved her own personal liberty with a willful rebellion against control. Perhaps I could have brought myself into the limitations of order and method in no other way. Like a plant that starts up in showers and sunshine and does not know which has best helped it to grow, it is difficult to say whether the hard things or the pleasant things did me most good. But when I was sincerest with myself, as also when I thought least about it, I know that I was glad to be alive, and to be just where I was.

After three years as a spinner she took a position as bookkeeper. She published several poems in *The Lowell Offering*, and although she spent many years as a schoolteacher in Illinois and Massachusetts before establishing her literary career, she went on to become the most highly regarded literary figure of the Lowell mills.

Larcom spent ten years in the mills before accompanying her sister Emmeline and her husband to Illinois in 1846. She supported herself as a teacher, first at a small school in a prairie community, then at Monticello Seminary near Alton, Illinois. She returned to Massachusetts in 1854 where she took up her duties as a teacher at Wheaton Seminary in Norton, Massachusetts. She continued to write poetry throughout these years, refining her style and honing her skills. However, she was never able to support herself wholly through writing. She became a sought after editor and even edited two volumes of poetry by John Greenleaf Whittier. Valuing her independence above all else, she never married.

Larcom became a national literary figure in 1854 when her poem "Call to Kansas," a powerful antislavery panegyric against the Kansas-Nebraska Act, won a national contest. From that point on she became one of antislavery's most powerful voices. Her first book of poetry was published in the same year, entitled, *Similitudes from Ocean Prairie*. In 1869 she published another volume of her poetry solidifying her fame. Her most famous book, however, was *A New England Girlhood* (1892), a memoir of her years as a mill girl. Her death in the following year made headline news in Boston newspapers.

FABRIC REQUIREMENTS

Cream & Red Mini-Print 4152-0111 for background
Green Tonal 4155-0116 for stems
Green and Red Floral 4158-0116 for leaves
Olive Floral 4151-0116 for leaves
Green Print 4157-0116 for leaves
Blue Print 4157-0150 for small flowers
Blue Floral 4151-0150 for small flowers
Red Floral 4151-0111 for large flower
Red Tonal 4155-0111 for large flower
Red Print 4157-0111 for large flower
Red & Blue Plaid 4161-0150 for flower center
Gold Floral One 4156-0132 for flower centers

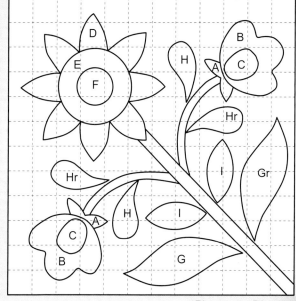

Placement Diagram

CUTTING DIRECTIONS

Use templates on pages 95-97

From the Cream & Red Mini-Print, cut: 8 – 13" squares
From the Green Tonal, cut: 2 – 1 1/2" x width of fabric (WOF) strips; 1 – 12" square; 16 – A
From the Green and Red Floral, cut: 8 each – G and Gr
From the Olive Floral, cut: 16 – I
From the Green Print, cut: 16 each – H and Hr
From both the Blue Print and the Blue Floral, cut: 8 – B
From the Red Tonal, cut: 8 – D
From both the Red Floral and Red Print, cut: 4 – D
From the Red & Blue Plaid, cut: 8 – E
From the Gold Floral One, fussy-cut: 16 – C and 8 –F, centering the floral motif

SEWING INSTRUCTIONS

1. Crease Cream & Red 13" square diagonally to create placement guides for appliqué.

2. From the Green 12" square, cut 1 1/4" bias strips. Join the strips together end-to-end to create continuous bias.

3. Curved Stems. Fold the 1 1/4" Green continuous bias strips from Step 2 in half lengthwise, wrong sides together. Stitch a scant ¼" from the raw edge. Insert the 3/8" bias pressing bar into the tube, centering the seam. Press seam to one side, trimming if necessary. Shift bias pressing bar a length at a time until the fabric tube is pressed flat. Cut into sixteen 5" long curved stem segments. Referring to the *Flower Block Placement Diagram*, position and secure in place with pins or dabs of glue and appliqué pieces to the background. *NOTE:* D flower template consists of four petals. Overlap and rotate two Ds made from 2 different red fabrics to create the flower).

4. Straight Stems. Fold the 1 1/2" x WOF wide Dark Green strips in half, wrong sides together. Stitch a scant 1/4" from the raw edge, then press using a 1/2" wide bias pressing bar. Cut into eight 10" stem segments. Position, secure in place, and appliqué pieces to the background.

5. Refer to the *Flower Block Placement Diagram* to position and secure remaining appliqué pieces. Using your method of choice, appliqué pieces to the background.

6. Make 4 blocks in Colorway One and 4 blocks in Colorway Two.

7. Press the blocks from the wrong side and trim to 12 1/2" square.

Block Six

FABRIC REQUIREMENTS

Cream Tonal 4154-0142
Ivory Tonal 4154-0140
Ivory Floral 4156-0140
Green & Red Floral 4158-0116
Olive Floral 4151-0116

CUTTING DIRECTIONS

From the Cream Tonal, cut: 20 – 2 7/8" B squares, cut in half once diagonally to make forty B triangles

From the Ivory Tonal, cut: 1 – 1 7/8" x 21" strip; 2 – 1 1/4" x 16" strips; 8 – 1 1/2" x 2 1/2" D rectangles

From the Ivory Floral, cut: 8 – 3 3/8" A squares; 4 – 2 7/8" squares, cut in half once diagonally to make eight B triangles

From the Green & Red Floral, cut: 1 – 1 7/8" x 16" strip; 8 – 2 7/8" B squares, cut in half once diagonally to make 16 B triangles; 2 – 2 1/2" C squares

From the Olive Floral, cut: 2 – 1 1/4" x 21" strips; 8 – 1 1/2" E squares

SEWING INSTRUCTIONS

1. Sew together the Olive Floral 1 1/4"-wide strips alternately with the Ivory Tonal 1 7/8" wide strips. Press seams toward Olive Floral. Cross-cut into 16 – 1 1/4"- wide segments.

2. Sew together the Ivory Tonal 1 1/4"-wide strips alternately with the Green & Red Floral 1 7/8" wide strip. Press seams toward Green & Red Floral. Crosscut into 8 – 1 7/8" wide segments.

3. Sew two of the segments made in step one, to opposite sides of one of the segments made in step two. Press seams open. Make a total of eight units.

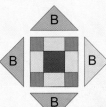

4. Sew 1 Ivory Floral B triangle and 3 Cream Tonal B triangles to each of the units. Make a total of eight units.

5. Lay out one Green & Red Floral C, four Ivory Tonal Ds, and four Olive Floral Es as shown. Sew patches together in rows, pressing seams toward the green fabrics. Sew together the rows. Repeat to make a total of two units.

6. Sew 2 Green & Red Floral B triangles and 2 Cream Tonal B triangles to an Ivory Floral A square. Make a total of eight units.

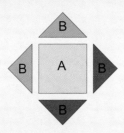

7. Referring to *Block Assembly Diagram*, arrange block units. Sew units together in rows; then, sew together the rows. Make a total of 2 blocks.

Block Assembly Diagram

Sabbath morning Aug 8th 47

Dear Elisabeth

I received your letter and perused it with the greatest pleasure imaginable. Still I envied you your comfort. I do wish I could be with you, would not I enjoy myself too? I'll bet I would. Now let me see what news have I got to write I cannot think of one item. O! yes I have been out sick two whole days. I was dreadful sick. I sewed all the time just as fast as my fingers would enable me to. You asked me about Marrilla. She is dead. She died at the Hospital the next morning after you left Lowell. Ruth Damon was with her when she asked her what she should tell her Father. Marrilla answered, "Tell him I die perfectly happy. I feel sure I shall see him in Heaven." I sincerely hope she will don't you? How bad to die so far away from all friends who care for you among those whose only wish is as seems to be to have you out of sight that they may get your money and clothes. Forgive me for speaking so bitterly. I could not help it for I think the treatments she received during her sickness was anything but fair, and when she died it was six o'clock in the morning and she was buried at two in the afternoon & I would just tell you another truth, but I dare not put it in black and white . . .

But I am writing all together differently from what I intended when I commenced this . . .

Everything else I like much better than I ever have elsewhere. I was thinking if you had any pigs they would have been set at liberty when you was eighteen. I wish I could have seen you that day. I should have given to something to remember I'll warrant you.

Mary L. Hovey

From the University of Massachusetts Lowell, Center for Lowell History

Block Seven

FINISHED SIZE: 12" x 12"

MAKE 2 BLOCKS

FABRIC REQUIREMENTS

Ivory Floral 4156-0140
Cream & Blue Floral 4154-0150
Ivory Tonal 4154-0140
Gold Floral One 4156-0132
Blue Print 4157-0150

CUTTING DIRECTIONS

From the Ivory Floral, cut: 8 – 3 3/8" A squares; 4 – 2 7/8" B squares
From the Cream & Blue Floral, cut: 16 – 2 7/8" B squares; 8 – 2 1/2" C squares
From the Ivory Tonal, cut: 8 – 2 7/8" B squares
From the Gold Floral One, cut: 8 – 2 7/8" B squares
From the Blue Print, cut: 2 – 3 3/8" A squares; 8 – 2 7/8" squares, cut in half once to make 16 D triangles

SEWING INSTRUCTIONS

1. Make half-square triangles by pairing an Ivory Floral B square and a Gold Floral One B square, right sides together. Draw a line diagonally from corner to corner on the wrong side of the Ivory Floral fabric. Sew 1/4" from both sides of the drawn line (*Diagram 1*). Cut on the drawn line and press toward the Gold Floral One fabric. Repeat for a total of 8 half-square triangles.

Diagram 1

2. Using the same method outlined in step one, make a total of 16 half-square triangles using the Cream & Blue Floral B squares and the Ivory Tonal B squares.

3. Arrange two Ivory Tonal/Cream & Blue half-square triangles, one Ivory Floral/Gold Floral One half-square triangle, and one Cream & Blue Floral C square as shown in *Diagram 2*. Sew units together. Repeat to make a total of 8 units.

Diagram 2

4. Cut the remaining Cream & Blue Floral B squares in half once diagonally to make 16 D triangles. Referring to *Diagram 3*, sew 2 Cream & Blue Floral D triangles to an Ivory Floral A square. Sew 2 Blue Print D triangles to complete the unit. Press all seams toward outside edge of unit. Make a total of eight units.

Diagram 3

5. Cut the remaining Gold Floral One squares in half to make 8 D triangles. Referring to *Diagram 4*, sew four D triangles to a Blue Print A square. Press seams toward outside edge. Repeat for a total of two units.

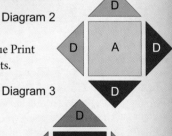

Diagram 4

6. Referring to *Block Assembly Diagram*, arrange block units. Sew units together in rows; then, sew together the rows. Make a total of 2 blocks.

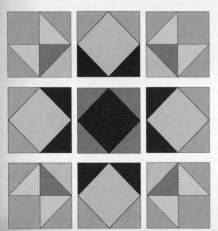

Block Assembly Diagram

39

Block Eight

FINISHED SIZE: 12" x 12"

MAKE 4 BLOCKS

FABRIC REQUIREMENTS

Ivory Floral 4156-0140
Cream & Blue Mini-Print 4152-0150
Brown & Blue Plaid 4161-0132
Gold Floral Two 4158-0132
Green Print 4157-0116
Green Tonal 4155-0116
Red Floral 4151-0111
Tan & Red Print 4423-0111

CUTTING DIRECTIONS

From the Ivory Floral, cut: 16 – 3 3/8" A squares; 8 – 2 7/8" B squares

From the Cream & Blue Mini-Print, cut: 32 – 2 7/8" B squares; 16 – 2 1/2" C squares

From the Brown & Blue Plaid, cut: 16 – 2 7/8" B squares

From the Gold Floral Two, cut: 8 – 2 7/8" B squares; 8 – 1 7/8" E squares

From the Green Print, cut: 8 – 2 7/8" squares, cut in half once diagonally to make 16 D triangles

From the Green Tonal, cut: 8 – 2 7/8" squares, cut in half once diagonally to make 16 D triangles

From the Red Floral, cut: 8 – 1 7/8" E squares

From the Tan & Red Print, cut: 8 – 2 7/8" squares, cut in half once diagonally to make 16 D triangles

SEWING INSTRUCTIONS

1. Make half-square triangles by pairing an Ivory Floral B square and a Gold Floral Two B square, right sides together. Draw a line diagonally from corner to corner on the wrong side of the Ivory Floral fabric. Sew 1/4" from both sides of the drawn line (*Diagram 1*). Cut on the drawn line and press toward the Gold Floral Two fabric. Repeat for a total of 16 half-square triangles.

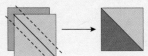

Diagram1

2. Using the same method outlined in step one, make a total of 32 half-square triangles using the Brown & Blue Plaid B squares and the Cream & Blue Mini-Print B squares.

3. Arrange two Brown & Blue Plaid/Cream & Blue Mini-Print half-square triangles, one Ivory Floral/Gold Floral Two half-square triangle, and one Cream & Blue Mini-Print C square as shown in *Diagram 2*. Sew units together. Repeat to make a total of 16 units.

Diagram 2

4. Cut the remaining Cream & Blue Mini-Print B squares in half once diagonally to make 32 D triangles. Referring to *Diagram 3*, sew 2 Cream & Blue Mini-Print D triangles to an Ivory Floral A square. Sew one Green Print D triangle and one Green Tonal D triangle to complete the unit. Press all seams toward outside edge of unit. Make a total of sixteen units.

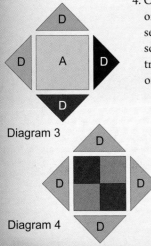

Diagram 3

Diagram 4

5. Make a Four-Patch with the Red Floral and Gold Floral Two E squares. Referring to *Diagram 4*, sew a Tan & Red Print D triangle to each side of the Four-Patch. Press seams toward outside edge. Make a total of four.

6. Referring to *Block Assembly Diagram*, arrange block units. Sew units together in rows; then sew the rows together. Make a total of 4 blocks.

Block Assembly Diagram

Block Nine

FINISHED SIZE: 12" x 12"

MAKE 4 BLOCKS

FABRIC REQUIREMENTS

Multi-color Floral 4149-0199
Ivory Tonal 4154-0140
Red Tonal 4155-0111
Red Floral 4151-0111
Tan & Red Print 4423-0111

CUTTING DIRECTIONS

From the Multi-color Floral, cut: 16 – 3 3/8" A squares; 8 – 2 7/8" squares, cut in half once diagonally to make 16 D triangles

From the Ivory Tonal, cut: 40 – 2 7/8" squares, cut in half once diagonally to make 80 D triangles

From the Red Tonal, cut: 16 – 2 7/8" squares, cut in half once diagonally to make 32 D triangles

From the Red Floral, cut: 4 – 4 1/2" C squares

From the Tan & Red Print, cut: 16 – 3 3/8" A squares

SEWING INSTRUCTIONS

1. Referring to *Diagram 1*, sew 1 Multi-color Floral D triangle to a Tan & Red Print A square. Sew 3 Ivory Tonal D triangles to complete the unit. Press all seams toward outside edge of unit. Make a total of 16 units.

2. Referring to *Diagram 2*, sew two Ivory Tonal D triangles and two Red Tonal D triangles to a Multi-color Floral A square. Press seams toward outside edge. Repeat for a total of 16 units.

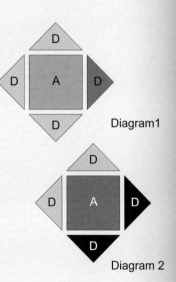

Diagram 1

Diagram 2

3. Referring to *Block Assembly Diagram*, arrange block units and Red Floral C square. Sew units together in rows; then, sew together the rows. Make a total of 4 blocks.

Block Assembly Diagram

43

Harriet Hanson Robinson:
From Mill Girl to Women's Rights Champion

Harriet Hanson Robinson was born in Boston, on August 2, 1825, the second of four children born to William and Harriet Hanson. When her father died, young Harriet was six years of age. Facing the daunting task of caring for four young children, Mrs. Hanson accepted her sister's invitation to move to Lowell to manage a boardinghouse for mill workers. Consequently, in 1832, the family traveled by boat up the Middlesex canal to the booming mill town.

In Lowell, Mrs. Hanson ran a house of forty boarders, and her daughter and namesake joined in the housework as did the other siblings. Young Harriet took up work in the mills at age ten to assist her family. Her first job was as a doffer – a worker who exchanged full bobbins from the spinning frame with empty ones. The job was considered appropriate for children because the work was easy, requiring only fifteen minutes of work per hour. During the off time the children were allowed to read, knit, or even go outside, during good weather, to play in the mill yard. Harriet worked on and off in the mills until the age of twenty-three. She left the mills for good when she married William Robinson on Thanksgiving Day in 1848. William Robinson was a political activist in the cause of antislavery and for a time published an antislavery newspaper. She had four children, one of whom died in infancy. She appeared to be content to live as a housewife and raise her children while her husband worked. After William's death, however, she became interested in the struggle for women's rights, and dedicated much of the rest of her life to the cause of women's suffrage.

She published the memoir of her life as a mill girl in 1898 when she was seventy-three. Her book *Loom and Spindle, or Life Among the Early Mill Girls*, portrayed life in the mills during the period of 1835 to 1848 at the height of Lowell's expansion and during the period when the "Lowell Experiment" was at its best. Some historians have chided Robinson for painting an overly idyllic picture of factory work, but she always claimed that she was accurate in describing her personal experience in the mills. Certainly Robinson's circumstances were more favorable than most, because she resided with her family and came to hold skilled jobs that permitted her the opportunity to read and participate in the many cultural opportunities that Lowell had to offer.

Robinson's last years were spent with her extended family, but she continued to read and write. Her hobby was sewing, which she continued to the very end of her life. At the age of eighty-six Harriet Hanson Robinson died on December 22, 1911. Her obituary appeared in several newspapers where she was lauded for her contributions as a champion of women's rights. During the bicentennial celebration in 1976, her family home in Malden was declared a landmark.

In *Loom and Spindle* she commented on the independence that money provided. "It is well to digress here a little, and speak of the influence the possession of money had on the characters of some of these women. We can hardly realize what a change the cotton factory made in the status of the working women. Hitherto woman had always been a money saving rather than a money earning, member of the community. Her labor could command but small return. If she worked out as servant, or "help," her wages were from 50 cents to $1.00 a week; or, if she went from house to house by the day to spin and weave, or do tailoress work, she could get but 75 cents a week and her meals. As teacher, her services were not in demand, and the arts, the professions, and even the trades and industries, were nearly all closed to her."

Block Ten

FINISHED SIZE: 12" x 12"

MAKE 4 BLOCKS

FABRIC REQUIREMENTS

Multi-color Floral 4149-0199
Ivory Tonal 4154-0140
Red Plaid 4160-0111
Blue Floral 4151-0150
Tan & Blue Print 4423-0150

CUTTING DIRECTIONS

From the Multi-color Floral, cut: 16 – 3 3/8" A squares; 8 – 2 7/8" squares, cut in half once diagonally to make 16 D triangles

From the Ivory Tonal, cut: 40 – 2 7/8" squares, cut in half once diagonally to make 80 D triangles

From the Red Plaid, cut: 16 – 2 7/8" squares, cut in half once diagonally to make 32 D triangles

From the Blue Floral, cut: 16 – 2 7/8" squares, cut in half once diagonally to make 32 D triangles

From the Tan & Blue Print, cut: 16 – 3 3/8" A squares

SEWING INSTRUCTIONS

1. Referring to *Diagram 1*, sew 1 Multi-color Floral D triangle to a Tan & Blue Print A square. Sew 3 Ivory Tonal D triangles to complete the unit. Press all seams toward outside edge of unit. Make a total of 16 units.

2. Referring to *Diagram 2*, sew two Ivory Tonal D triangles, a Red Plaid D triangle, and Blue Floral D triangle to a Multi-color Floral A square. Press seams toward outside edge. Repeat for a total of 16 units.

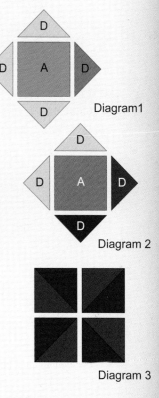

Diagram 1

Diagram 2

Diagram 3

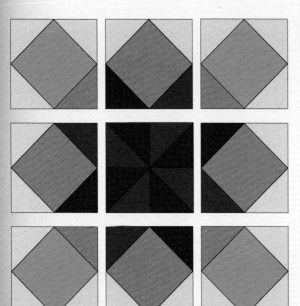

3. Sew 4 Red Plaid and 4 Blue Floral D triangles together to make half-square triangles. Then, sew the half-square triangles together in a Pinwheel block as shown in *Diagram 3*. Make a total of four.

4. Referring to *Block Assembly Diagram* arrange block units. Sew units together in rows; then, sew together the rows. Make a total of 4 blocks.

Block Assembly Diagram

ASSEMBLING THE QUILT

Fabric Requirements
Red Tonal 4155-0111
Brown Tonal 4155-0113
Stripe 4148-0199
Assorted Fabric from Quilt

CUTTING DIRECTIONS

From the Red Tonal, cut: 2 – 3 1/2" x 40 1/2" top/bottom borders; 3 – 3 1/2" x WOF strips, pieced together end-to-end and recut into 2 – 3 1/2" x 46 1/2" side borders; 11 – 2 1/4" x WOF strips, pieced together end-to-end for binding

From the Brown Tonal, cut: 6 – 3 1/2" x WOF strips, pieced together end-to-end and recut into 2 – 3 1/2" x 54 1/2" side borders and 2 – 3 1/2" x 60 1/2" top/bottom borders; 9 – 2 1/2" x WOF strips, pieced together end-to-end and recut into 2 – 2 1/2" x 84 1/2" side borders and 2 – 2 1/2" x 88 1/2" top/bottom borders

From the Stripe, cut: 10 – 6 1/2" x WOF strips, pieced together end-to-end, matching stripe pattern. Recut into 2 – 6 1/2" x 88 1/2" side borders and 2 – 6 1/2" x 100 1/2" top/bottom borders.

From the Assorted Fabric from Quilt, cut: 184 – 2 1/2" A squares

SEWING INSTRUCTIONS
Refer to *Quilt Assembly Diagram* on pg 48

1. Sew together Bock One and Block Two. Press seams open.

2. Sew a Block Three and a Reversed Block Three to sides, pressing seams open.

3. Sew **Spool Block Borders** to top and bottom of quilt center. Press seams toward borders.

4. **Border One.** Sew the Red Tonal 3 1/2" x 40 1/2" borders to top and bottom of quilt. Sew the remaining Red Tonal borders to quilt sides. Press seams toward borders.

5. **Border Two.** Sew the Assorted Fabric A squares together randomly into pairs. Set aside 4 pairs and sew the remaining pairs together into 44 Four Patch blocks. Assemble the Four Patch blocks into 4 borders of 10 blocks each. You should have 4 blocks remaining. Sew one of the pairs you set aside onto the end of each of the borders. Sew a border to each side of the quilt. Press seams toward quilt center. Sew a Four Patch block each end of the remaining two borders. Sew to top and bottom of quilt. Press seams toward quilt center.

6. **Border Three.** Sew a Brown Tonal 3 1/2" x 54 1/2" border to each side of the quilt. Sew remaining 3 1/2" wide Brown Tonal borders to the top and bottom. Press seams toward borders.

7. **Border Four.** Arrange the pieced blocks as shown in the *Quilt Assembly Diagram*, making sure blocks are oriented correctly. Sew borders to quilt.

8. **Border Five.** Sew the Brown Tonal 2 1/2" x 84 1/2" borders to sides of quilt. Add remaining Brown Tonal borders to top and bottom of quilt. Press all seams toward borders.

9. **Border Six.** Sew the 6 1/2" x 88 1/2" long borders to sides of quilt. Add the remaining stripe borders to top and bottom of quilt. Press all seams toward quilt center.

FINISHING

1. Layer top, batting, and backing. Quilt as desired.

2. Use the Red Tonal 2 1/4" binding strips to finish the quilt.

AWAY FROM HOME
QUILT ASSEMBLY DIAGRAM

Border Six 6 ½″ x 100 ½″

Border Five 2 ½″ x 88 ½″

| Block 7 | Block 10 | Block 5 Left | Block 8 | Block 5 Right | Block 9 | Block 6 |

Border Three 3 ½″ x 60 ½″

Block 9

Border One 3 ½″ x 40 ½″

Block 10

Block 5 Right

Block 5 Left

Block 2

3 ½″ x 54 ½″

3 ½″ x 46 ½″

Block 3

Block 3r

3 ½″ x 46 ½″

3 ½″ x 54 ½″

Block 8

Block 1

Block 8

Block 5 Left

3 ½″ x 40 ½″

Block 5 Right

Block 10

3 ½″ x 60 ½″

Block 9

| Block 6 | Block 9 | Block 5 Right | Block 8 | Block 5 Left | Block 10 | Block 7 |

Border Five 2 ½″ x 84 ½″

Border Six 6 ½″ x 88 ½″

Border Five 2 ½″ x 88 ½″

Stars Aplenty

FINISHED QUILT SIZE: 74" x 85 1/2"

FINISHED BLOCK SIZE: 10" x 10"

DESIGNED, STITCHED, AND QUILTED BY NANCY RINK

MAKE 30 BLOCKS

FABRIC REQUIREMENTS

1 fat quarter each of 14 assorted Red & Blue Print fabrics for blocks
1 yard Red Tonal for blocks and binding
1/2 yard Beige Floral for blocks
3 yards Beige Dot for sashing and borders
1 7/8 yards Multi-color Stripe for outer border
5 1/3 yards for backing

CUTTING DIRECTIONS

This quilt has a great scrappy look to it and is a great way to use a collection of fat quarters. From each of the 14 fat quarters you'll be cutting enough patches for two blocks. This will yield 28 of the thirty blocks needed to complete the quilt. The remaining two blocks are cut from the same red tonal fabric that is used for the binding. Also, you will only need a total of 20 G patches, although you will cut 28. This gives you a little freedom to move the Gs around when laying out the quilt.

From *each* Red & Blue Print fat quarter cut
(see *Fat Quarter Cutting Diagram*):
    2 – 3 1/8" x 3 1/8" A squares
    8 – 2 3/4" x 2 3/4" squares, cut in half once diagonally to make 16 B triangles
    4 – 1 3/4" x 8" E rectangles
    4 – 1 3/4" x 10 1/2" F rectangles
    2 – 2" x 2" G squares

From the Red Tonal cut:
    9 – 2 1/4" x WOF strips, pieced together end-to-end for binding
    2 – 3 1/8" x 3 1/8" A squares
    8 – 2 3/4" x 2 3/4" squares, cut in half once diagonally to make 16 B triangles
    4 – 1 3/4" x 8" E rectangles
    4 – 1 3/4" x 10 1/2" F rectangles
    2 – 2" x 2" G squares

From the Beige Floral cut: 60 – 2 3/4" x 2 3/4" squares, cut in half once diagonally to make 120 B triangles

From the Beige Dot cut:
    7 – 3 1/2" X WOF strips, pieced end-to-end and recut into 2 – 3 1/2" x 62 1/2") top/bottom borders and 2 – 3 1/2" x 68" side borders
    3 – 10 1/2" x WOF strips, recut into 49 – 2" x 10 1/2" sashing strips
    4 – 5" x WOF strips, recut into 30 – 5" x 5" squares, cut in half twice diagonally to make 120 C triangles
    8 – 2 3/8" x WOF strips, recut into 120 – 2 3/8" x 2 3/8" D squares

From the Multi-color Stripe cut:
    8 – 6 1/2" x WOF strips, pieced together end to end and recut into 2 – 6 1/2" x 74" side borders and 2 – 6 1/2" x 74 1/2" top/bottom borders

From the Backing cut: 2 – 91" x WOF panels

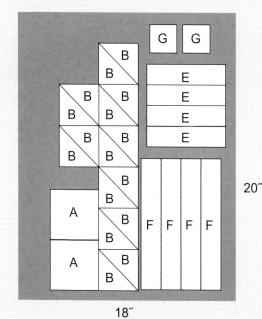

Fat Quarter Cutting Diagram

SEWING INSTRUCTIONS
FRAMED STAR BLOCK

1. To make one block, gather a matching set of 1 A, 8 B, 2 E, and 2 F patches.

2. Sew four Beige Floral B triangles to a Red & Blue print fabric A Square to create a Square-in-a-Square as shown in *Diagram 1*. Press seams toward center of block.

Diagram 1

3. Sew a Red & Blue print fabric B triangle on to either side of a Beige Dot C triangle to create a Flying Geese unit as shown in *Diagram 2*. Make a total of four matching Flying Geese units.

Diagram 2
Make 4 matching
Flying Geese units

4. Lay out units made in steps one and two and 4 Beige Dot patches as shown in *Diagram 3*. Sew together into rows, then sew together the rows.

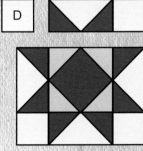

Diagram 3

5. Add two Red & Blue print fabric E rectangles to opposite sides of block. Press seams toward rectangles. Add the F Red & Blue print fabric rectangles to the remaining sides of the block (*Diagram 4*).

Diagram 4

6. Repeat process to make a total of 30 blocks.

ASSEMBLING THE QUILT

1. Referring to the *Quilt Assembly Diagram*, lay out the blocks alternately with Beige Dot sashing strips. You should have six rows of five blocks each. Lay out the sash rows by alternating various Red & Blue Print G pieces and sashing strips.

2. Sew the block rows to the sashing rows (see *Quilt Assembly Diagram*). Press all seams toward sashing.

3. Sew the Beige Dot 3 1/2" x 68" borders to the sides of the quilt. Press seams toward borders. Add the remaining Beige Dot borders to top and bottom of quilt, again pressing seams toward borders.

4. Sew the Multi-color Stripe 6 1/2" x 74" borders to the sides of the quilt; add the remaining Multi-color Stripe borders to top and bottom of quilt. Press all seams toward outside edge.

FINISHING

1. Sew together the two backing panels and press seam open.

2. Layer quilt top, batting, and backing. Quilt as desired.

3. Trim batting and backing even with edge of quilt.

4. Use the Red Tonal 2 1/4" binding strips to finish the quilt.

Quilt Assemnbly Diagram

Flowers in the Mills

FINISHED QUILT SIZE: 54 1/4" x 54 1/4"

FINISHED BLOCK NUMBER AND SIZE:
1 – 29 1/2" x 29 1/2" AND 20 – 5 1/8" x 5 1/8"

DESIGNED, STITCHED, AND QUILTED BY NANCY RINK

FABRIC REQUIREMENTS

1 yard Cream Solid or Muslin for center appliqué
   block background
1/2 yard Cream Print for pieced star block background
1 3/4 yards Cream Multi-print for border #2
10 fat quarters of coordinating fabrics for appliqués, pieced
   star blocks, and pieced outer border
12" square Red & Brown Stripe for basket appliqué
Fat eighth Olive Green Texture #1 for appliqué leaves
8" square Olive Green Texture #2 for appliqué leaves
1/2 yard Dark Green Print for bias stems and appliqué leaves
1/2 yard Light Brown Texture for setting triangles
1/2 yard Light Brown Print for setting triangles
1/2 yard Brown Print for binding
3 1/2 yards for backing

SUPPLIES

Fusible Web (optional)
Bias Press Bars
Stabilizer for machine appliqué
28 wt. Black # 2692 Aurifil thread for machine buttonhole stitch
or DMC #310 Black Embroidery Floss for hand buttonhole stitch

CUTTING DIRECTIONS

Use appliqué templates on pages 98-102

From the Cream Solid or Muslin, cut: 1 – 30" square

From the Cream Print, cut: 4 – 2" x WOF strips, recut into 80 –
   2" P squares; 2 – 3 3/8" x WOF strips, recut into 20 – 3 3/8"
   squares, cut in half twice diagonally to make 80 – O triangles

*From the Cream Multi-print, cut: 2 – 4 1/8" x 44" side borders;
   2 – 4 1/8" x 51 1/4" top/bottom borders

   *Do not cut until step 7. These measurements are mathemati-
   cally correct. Depending on differences in sewing technique, you
   may need to cut these according to the actual measurement of
   your quilt.

From the 10 fat quarters of coordinating fabrics, cut: 4 – N
   diamonds (template on pg. 86) from each of the fat quarters;
   1 – 2 1/4" x 20 to 21"-long strip from each of the fat quarters for
   outer border

Refer to the photo of the quilt for color placement and cut a total
   of: 6 F Berries; 9 G Flowers; 12 H Flowers/ Flower Centers; 4 J
   Buds; 4 K Calyxes; and 3 M Circle Flower Centers.

From the Red & Brown Stripe, cut: 1 each B and BR basket
   handles; 1 C basket

From the Olive Green Texture #1, cut: 1 D leaf; 1 I leaf; 1 IR leaf;
   5 E leaves; 2 L leaves

From the Olive Green Texture #2, cut: 1 I leaf; 3 E leaves; 1 L leaf

From the Dark Green Print, cut: 5 – 2" x 20" bias strips;
   1 – D leaf; 1 – DR leaf; 1 – IR leaf; 5 – E leaves; 1 – L leaf

From the Light Brown Texture, cut: 4 – 8 1/2" squares, cut in half
   twice diagonally to make 16 Q triangles; 6 – 4 1/2" squares,
   cut in half once diagonally to make 12 R triangles

From the Light Brown Print, cut: 4 – 8 1/2" squares, cut in half
   twice diagonally to make 2 Q triangles; 6 – 4 1/2" squares,
   cut in half once diagonally to make 4 R triangles

From the Brown Print, cut: 6 – 2 1/4" x WOF strips, pieced
   end-to-end for binding

From the Backing, cut: 2 – 30" x 59" panels; 1 – 9" x 54
   hanging sleeve

Lowell, 1840

In the mills, we are not so far from God and nature, as many persons might suppose. We cultivate and enjoy much pleasure in cultivating flowers and plants. A large and beautiful variety of plants is placed around the walls of the rooms, giving them more the appearance of a flower garden than a workshop. It is there we inhale the sweet perfume of the rose, the lily, and geranium; and, with them send the sweet incense of sincere gratitude to the bountiful Giver of these rich blessings.

Sarah G. Begley

SEWING INSTRUCTIONS

Appliqué the Center Panel A

Note: The appliqué in the quilt shown was completed with fusible web. To do the same, trace shapes onto the paper side of fusible web. Although most of the appliqué patches are symmetrical, some are not and may require reversing. To reduce bulk and stiffness, the center area of the fusible web was cut away from the shapes prior to fusing.

1. Refer to the *Appliqué Placement Guide* for positioning your appliqué pieces. You may wish to make a placement guide using 1" grid paper, and then trace the appliqué pieces. Or, you may just "eyeball" the placement of the pieces. This will give your piece a true folk art charm.

2. Using the appliqué method of your choice, appliqué the pieces in place, beginning first with the stems.

3. To prepare the Dark Green Print stems for appliqué, fold strips in half lengthwise, wrong sides together. Stitch a scant 1/4" from the raw edge. Insert the 3/4" Bias Press Bar into the tube, centering the seam. Press seam to one side, trimming if necessary. Shift Bias Press Bar a length at a time until all fabric tubes are pressed flat.

4. Cut the following stem lengths:

   1 stem 20" long
   2 stems 12" long
   2 stems 9" long
   2 stems 8 1/2" long
   2 stems 6" long
   2 stems 4 1/2" long

5. In the quilt shown, the appliqué was fused in place using a fusible web, and then the edges of the appliqué were finished with a decorative machine blanket stitch done in black thread. However, if you are appliquéing the pieces by hand, then use black embroidery thread to complete the decorative blanket stitch.

6. After the appliqué is complete, press center panel from the wrong side and trim to 29 1/2" x 29 1/2".

▲ Center

= 1"   Appliqué Placement Diagram

BORDERS

BORDER ONE

1. Each block in Border One is made with eight N pieces, 4 of which are one color and 4 of which are another color. Referring to the *Block-Piecing Diagram*, make four sets of N/N patches for each star. Sew the N/N's together as shown and then set in the Cream Print O and P patches. Make 20 blocks.

Block Piecing Diagram
Make 20

We have been greatly pleased with the taste and care displayed in the introduction and culture of plants and flowers, on all the Corporations... It is especially gratifying to behold them thriving beneath the kindly care of the female operative in our factories. In the dressing room of No. 3 on the Boott Corporation, we counted over 200 pots of plants and flowers!

A few suggestions may not be considered out of place... Let the flowers and plants be carefully attended to. Lessons of wisdom, purity, and holt trust, will thence be derived. And when you look on such as you brought from "home," remember the love of your kindred and the joys of your childhood; and haply your thoughts will be in harmony with the teaching of flowers as "the alphabet of angels."

Excerpted from The Lowell Offering

2. Notice that the Light Brown print is on the inner edges of the Border One strip and that the Light Brown Texture is on the outside. Referring to the *Quilt Assembly Diagram*, join the blocks with the R and Q patches to make the side, top, and bottom strips. First join the side border strips to center panel A, then add the top and bottom strips.

BORDER TWO

1. Measure through the center of the quilt before attaching the Cream Multi-print Border Two pieces. Cut your border pieces 4 1/8" wide x the measurement of your quilt. Attach the Cream Multi-print Border Two side strips to the quilt. In the same manner, measure, cut, and then attach the Border Two top and bottom strips.

BORDER THREE

1. Using the assorted 2 1/4" strips cut from the ten fat quarters, sew them together randomly to make strip panels. Use no more than five strips in each panel. Crosscut into 2 1/4"-wide strips. (*Diagram 1*)

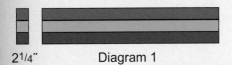

2¼"   Diagram 1

2. Sew together the strips so that 29 squares form the side border strips, and 31 squares form the top and bottom strips. Attach the pieced border strips to the quilt. Press seams toward quilt center.

FINISHING

1. Sew together backing panels, pressing seams open.

2. Layer backing, batting, and quilt top. Quilt as desired.

3. Use the Brown Print 2 1/4" binding strips to finish the quilt.

4. To make the hanging sleeve, turn under 1/2" twice on each short end of the 9" x 54" strip cut from the backing fabric and press. Stitch hem in place. Fold in half lengthwise, wrong sides together. Stitch 1/2" from raw edge, back stitching to secure seams. Press seam open, centering it on the "back" side of the hanging sleeve tube. Center sleeve approximately 1/2" from top edge of quilt back, making sure the seam is against the quilt back. Whipstitch the sleeve in place being careful not to sew through to the quilt front. Leave "top" edge of tube ends open to allow a hanging rod to be inserted.

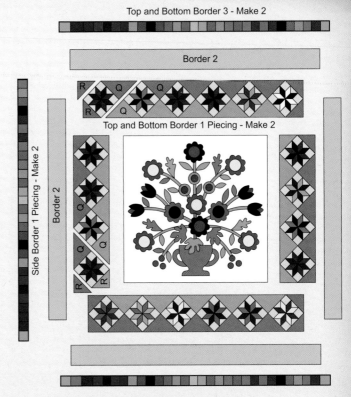

Quilt Assemnbly Diagram

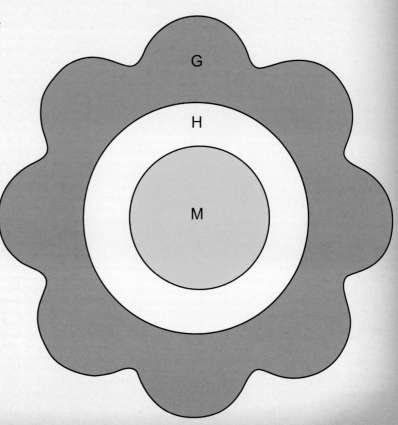

Lowell, 1844

Dear Mary,

    Then the girls dress so neatly, and are so pretty. The mill girls are the prettiest in the city. You wonder how they can keep neat. Why not? There are no restrictions as to the number of pieces to be washed in the boarding house. And, as there is plenty of water in the mill, the girls can wash their laces and muslins and other nice things themselves, and no boarding woman ever refuses the conveniences for starching and ironing.

    You ask me how the girls behave in the mill, and what are the punishments. They behave very well while about their work, and I have never heard of punishments, or scoldings, or anything of that sort. Sometimes an overseer finds fault, and sometimes offends a girl by refusing to let her stay out of the mill, or some deprivation like that; and then, perhaps, there are tears and pouts on her part, but, in general, the tone of intercourse between the girls and overseers is very good—pleasant, yet respectful. . . .

                        Yours always,

                        Susan

Excerpted from The Lowell Offering

Lovely Ladies

FINISHED QUILT SIZE: 73" x 73"

FINISHED BLOCK SIZE: 14"x 14" ✦ MAKE 9 BLOCKS

DESIGNED AND STITCHED BY NANCY RINK

QUILTED BY CHRISTIANE MARZI

FABRIC REQUIREMENTS

3/8 yard Green Floral for appliqué
2/3 yard Green Print for appliqué
5/8 yard Red Floral for appliqué
7/8 yard Red Texture for appliqué and binding
1 3/4 yards Ivory Tonal for sashing
2 1/4 yards Tan Print for appliqué block background
2 3/4 yards Black Large Floral
4 7/8 yards Backing fabric for appliqué, block frames, and border

SUPPLIES

Bias Press Bars
Perfect Circles® by Karen Kay Buckley (optional)
Bigger Perfect Circles® by Karen Kay Buckley (optional)
Thread to match appliqué patches

Lovely Ladies was constructed using the freezer paper and starch appliqué method. The following supplies are recommended if you plan to use the same method.
Freezer Paper
Mary Ellen's Best Press Liquid Starch
Artist's Brush
Mini-Iron
Awl/Chopstick
Fabric Glue

CUTTING DIRECTIONS

Use appliqué templates on pages 103-104

From the Green Floral, cut: 16 – B calyxes; 32 – D leaves
From the Green Print, cut: 4 – 1 1/4" x WOF strips;
   20 – B calyxes; 40 – D leaves
From the Red Floral, cut: 72 – C leaves; 25 – E circles
From the Red Texture, cut: 36 – A buds; 8 – 2 1/4" x WOF strips
   pieced end-to-end for binding
From the Ivory Tonal, cut: 3 – 14 1/2" x WOF strips, recut into
   24 – 4 1/2" x 14 1/2" G rectangles; 2 – 5" x WOF strips, recut
   into 16 – 5" I squares
From the Tan Print, cut: 9 – 15" squares
From the Black Large Floral, cut: 2 – 8" x 58 1/2" side borders,
   cut parallel to selvedge; 2 – 8" x 73 1/2" top/bottom borders,
   cut parallel to selvedge; 36 – H Block Frames; 25 – F Circles
From the Backing fabric, cut: 2 – 81" x WOF panels

SEWING INSTRUCTIONS

LOVELY LADIES APPLIQUE BLOCK

1. If desired, create an appliqué block placement guide by folding a 14" square of freezer paper in quart ers. Trace the pattern onto one quarter. Reposition the freezer paper and trace the remaining quarter blocks to create a full block pattern. (*Left*)

2. To prepare the Green Print stems for appliquéing, fold the 1 1/4"-wide strips in half lengthwise, wrong sides together. Stitch a scant 1/4" from the raw edge. Insert the 3/8" Bias Press Bar into the tube, centering the seam. Press seam to one side, trimming if necessary. Shift Bias Press Bar a length at a time until all fabric tubes are pressed flat.

3. Cut the Green Print stem strips into 36 – 3 3/4" long pieces.

4. If desired, use the *Perfect Circles* and *Bigger Perfect Circles* templates in sizes that correspond with the E and F circles to prepare these pieces for appliqué.

4. Fold and crease the Tan Print squares vertically, horizontally, and diagonally to create placement guides for appliqué.

5. Using the appliqué method of your choice, appliqué the pieces in place, beginning first with the stems. Then, appliqué pieces in place in alphabetical order according to Appliqué Placement Guide.

6. Make four blocks with the Green Floral B and D pieces and five blocks with the Green Print B and D pieces.

7. Press blocks from wrong side and trim to 14 1/2" square.

Appliqué Placement Guide

SASHING STRIPS

Use appliqué template H on page 104.

1. Appliqué Black Large Floral H Block Frames onto one side of 12 Ivory Tonal G rectangles as shown in *Diagram 1*.

Diagram 1

2. Appliqué Black Large Floral H Block Frames onto two sides of 12 Ivory Tonal G rectangles as shown in *Diagram 2*.

Diagram 2

CORNERSTONES

1. If desired, use the *Perfect Circles* and *Bigger Perfect Circles* templates in sizes that correspond with the E and F circles to prepare these pieces for appliqué.

2. Fold and crease Ivory Tonal I squares horizontally and vertically to create placement lines for appliqué.

3. Appliqué Red Floral E and Black Large Floral F pieces to Ivory Tonal I squares (*Diagram 3*). Make a total of 16 blocks.

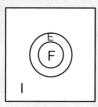

Diagram 3

4. Press blocks from wrong side and trim to 4 1/2" square.

ASSEMBLING THE QUILT

1. Lay out the Lovely Lady blocks, the sashing strips, and the cornerstones as shown in the *Quilt Assembly Diagram*.

2. **Sash Rows.** Sew together the sashing strips together alternately with the cornerstones. Press seams toward cornerstones.

3. **Block Rows.** Sew the Lovely Lady blocks together alternately with the sashing strips. Press seams toward blocks.

4. Sew together Sash Rows and Block Rows. Press seams toward blocks.

BORDERS

1. Sew the Black Large Floral 8" x 58 1/2" borders to sides of quilt. Press seams toward borders.

2. Sew the remaining Black Large Floral borders to top/bottom of quilt. Press seams toward borders.

FINISHING

1. Sew together backing panels, pressing seams open.

2. Layer backing, batting, and quilt top. Quilt as desired.

3. Trim batting and backing even with edge of quilt.

4. Use the Red Texture 2 1/4" binding strips to finish the quilt

Quilt Assembly Diagram

April 15, 1843

TO THE BRETHREN & SISTERS OF THE JOHN ST. CHURCH

Dearly Beloved,

I feel it to be my duty to make a communication to you, acknowledging, where in I have sinned, and done wrong, dishonored my savior, it brought a disgrace upon his cause which I have professed to love for which I am truly sorry and ask to be forgiven both by the church and its great Head.

To save my reputation as a weaver, I have taken the ticket from cloth woven by another person and placed it upon that done by myself, which was imperfect; and put my ticket upon hers – thereby practicing dishonesty, and sinning against God and the church, and dishonoring the Christian name.

While I would make acknowledgment to the church and ask to be forgiven, I would also ask to be remembered in their prayers, that I may hereafter be kept from evil, and the appearance of it, and live as becomeths a disciple of a perfect Savior.

Sarah White

From the University of Massachusetts Lowell, Center for Lowell History

Busy Weaver

Finished Size: 46" x 46"

Finished block size: 14" x 14"; make 4 blocks

Designed, stitched and quilted by Nancy Rink

FABRIC REQUIREMENTS

This quilt began with a packet of fat quarters of various fabrics from Judie Rothermel's *A Journey Through Time* collection. The border fabrics were then added to complete the palette for the quilt. A and B patches were added to the blocks from the Blue Border fabric. Mix and match the fabrics to achieve the scrappy look of the quilt.

1 yard or 4 fat quarters of light print
1 1/4 yds *total* or 5 fat quarters of red, blue, gold, and brown coordinating prints
3/4 yd of blue border print
3/8 yd of red stripe
1/2 yard of binding fabric

CUTTING DIRECTIONS

From the light print(s) cut: a total of
16 – 2 1/2" A squares; 32 – 2 7/8" B squares; 2 – 2 1/2" x 14 1/2" C strips; 3 – 2 1/2" x 30 1/2" D strips; and 2 – 2 1/2" x 34 1/2" E strips

From the red, blue, gold, and brown coordinating prints cut: a total of (use the blue border print after cutting G strips, if desired):
116 – 2 1/2" A squares; 32 – 2 7/8" B squares; 4 – 4 1/2" H squares

From the Blue Border print cut:
4 – 4 1/2" x 38 1/2" G strips

From the Red Stripe cut:
2 – 2 1/2" x 34 1/2" E strips;
2 – 2 1/2" x 38 1/2" F strips

From the binding fabric cut:
5 – 2 1/4" x WOF" strips, pieced together end-to-end for binding

SEWING INSTRUCTIONS

BUSY WEAVER BLOCK

Note: Study the fabric placement in the block. Different looks are achieved by placing the darker, stronger colors in different positions in the block.

1. For one block, gather 4 light print A patches, 8 light print B patches, 29 various print A patches, and 8 various print B patches.

2. Pair the 8 light print B patches with 8 matching B patches of one of the prints. Place right sides together. Draw a line diagonally from corner to corner. Stitch ¼ inch from both sides of drawn line. Cut on drawn line and press to the dark fabric. Lay out patches in the position indicated in the *Block Assembly Diagram*. Sew patches together in rows; then sew the rows together. Make a total of four blocks.

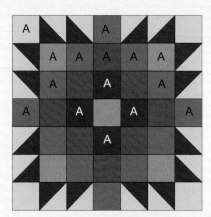

Block Assembly Diagram

ASSEMBLING THE QUILT

1. Lay out the four blocks and the C, D, and E light print strips. Refer to the *Quilt Assembly Diagram* for placement.

2. Sew two blocks together with a C strip in the middle between the two blocks. Press seams toward C strip. Next, sew these sections together with a D strip. Add the remaining D strips to the top and bottom of the quilt. Press seams toward D strips. Add E strips to quilt sides, pressing seams toward E strips.

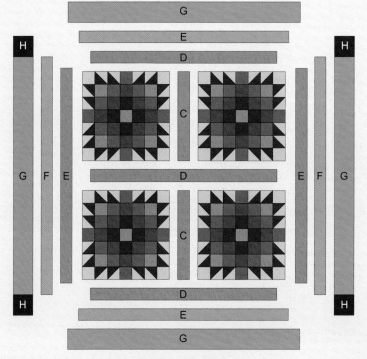

Quilt Assembly Diagram

BORDERS

BORDER ONE. Sew Red Stripe E strips to top and bottom of quilt. Add F strips to sides. Press all seams toward Red Stripe border.

BORDER TWO. Sew the Blue Border print G strips to top and bottom of quilt. Sew the H squares to the ends of the two remaining G strips. Add these borders to quilt sides.

FINISHING

1. Layer top, batting and backing. Quilt as desired.

2. Use the 2 1/4" binding strips to finish the quilt.

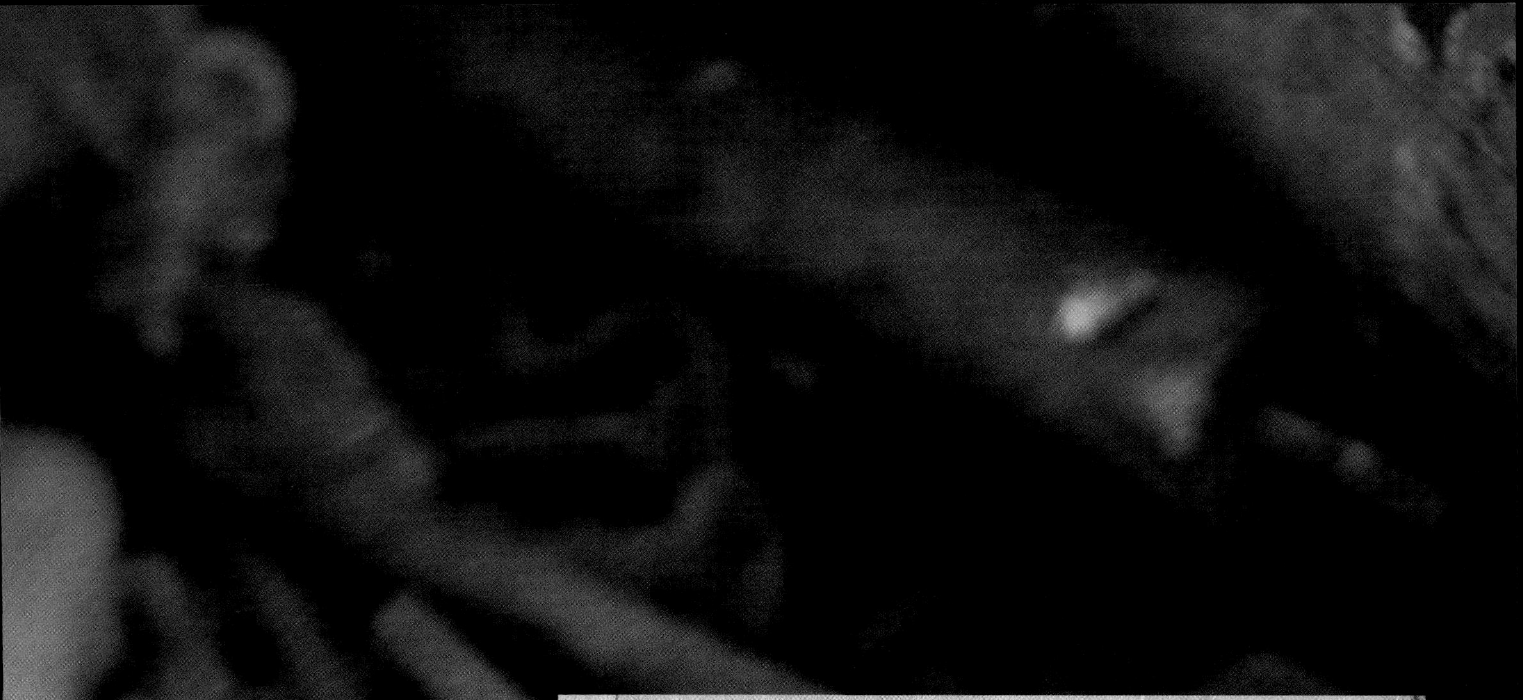

Lowell, Dec 15, 1850

Dear Mother,

I received your kind letter and Hellens both in the same day and read them with feelings which can better be imagined than described...

It may seem strange that I do not board on the corporation on which I am working but I have some very warm friends at Mrs. Thomas that I want to stay with.. Peirce is here and sends her love to you. She is one of the kindest old ladies you ever seing. She is a mother to me and I do not know how I should get along without her.

Well I suppose Christmas is close upon us and I hope it will be welcomed with joy as the birth day of our redeemer. You and Father must sing "While Shepherds Watch their flocks by night" and think I am joining you for I shall remember all the good old times that we have had together . . . I shall probably stay another year if I am well. I want you should find out how much it will cost to get an adition built for you, but you must get some man to take hold of it for you, one that will go ahead and make good calculer. I wish uncle George would do the calculating. He is the best one that I can think of . . for I am confident that Lealand [her brother] will never do anything about it. If he cannot keep himself cloathed he certainly cannot think of building houses. I will send you one hundred dollars in one year.

If you can get along for provisions and wood without my help I shall be able to lay up the most of [my] wages which will amount to something like 9 dollars per month. The year round I shall put it in the bank whare it will gain a little.

Give my love and thanks to Aunt Lucy and all the friends that you may see

Amy Melenda Galusha

From the Lowell National Historical Park Galusha Family Collection

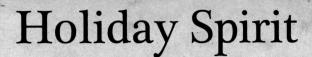

Holiday Spirit

FINISHED BLOCK SIZE: 24" SQUARE
FINISHED QUILT SIZE: 34" x 34"
DESIGNED AND STITCHED BY NANCY RINK
QUILTED BY CHRISTIANE MARZI

FABRIC REQUIREMENTS

Style numbers refer to *The Mill Girls: 1830-1850* by Judie Rothermel for Marcus Fabrics. See swatches on page 21.

Fat Eighth of Cream Tonal 4154-0142 for appliqué
Fat Eighth of Tan & Red Print 4423-0111for appliqué
Fat Quarter of Gold Floral One 4156-0132 for appliqué
5/8 yard Green and Red Floral 4158-0116 for borders
7/8 yard Ivory Tonal 4154-0140 for appliqué and inner border
1-1/8 yards Red Tonal 4155-0111 for block background

SUPPLIES

Bias Pressing Bars
Fabric Glue
Thread to match appliqué
DMC Embroidery Floss, colors Ultra Lt. Mocha Brown 3866, Lt.
Hazelnut Brown 422, Hazelnut Brown 3828, Dk Rosewood 3857
for buttonhole and decorative stitches

CUTTING DIRECTIONS

Use Block Five templates from page 95-97

From the Cream Tonal cut: 8 – I; 8 – H and Hr
From the Tan & Red Print cut: 8 – C; 5 – F
From the Gold Floral One cut: 10 – D; 8 – B
From the Green & Red Floral cut: 2 – 4 1/2" x 26 1/2" side
    borders; 2 – 4 1/2" x 34 1/2" top/bottom borders
From the Ivory Tonal cut: 2 – 1 1/2" x 24 1/2" border;
    2 – 1 1/2" x 26 1/2" borders; 1– 1 1/2" x WOF" strips;
    1 – 10" square; 8 – A; 5 – E; and 4 – G and Gr
From the Red Tonal cut: 1 – 25" square; 4 – 2 1/4" x WOF strips
    for binding

SEWING INSTRUCTIONS

All appliqué pieces were finished with a buttonhole stitch using embroidery floss. Additional decorative stitches were added around the flower centers.

Block Placement Diagram

1. Crease Red Tonal 25" square horizontally, vertically and diagonally to create placement guides for appliqué.

2. From the Ivory Tonal 10" square cut 1 1/4"-wide strips on the bias. Join strips together end-to-end to create continuous bias.

3. **Curved Stems.** To prepare the Ivory Tonal continuous bias for appliqué, fold the 1 1/4"-wide strips in half lengthwise, wrong sides together. Stitch a scant 1/4" from the raw edge. Insert the 3/8" bias pressing bar into the tube, centering the seam. Press seam to one side, trimming if necessary. Shift bias pressing bar a length at a time until the fabric tube is pressed flat. Cut into eight 5" long curved stem segments. Referring to the *Block Placement Diagram*, on page 33, position and secure with pins or dabs of glue and appliqué pieces to the background.

4. Fold the 1 1/2" x WOF wide Ivory Tonal strip in half, wrong sides together. Stitch a scant 1/4" from the raw edge, then, press using a 1/2" wide bias pressing bar. Cut into four 10"-long stem segments. Position, secure in place and appliqué pieces to the background.

5. Position and secure remaining appliqué pieces. Using method of choice, appliqué pieces to the background.

6. If desired, embroider additional decorative details around flower centers. In the quilt shown, straight stitches in various lengths radiate from the center circle and are tipped by French knots.

7. Press block from wrong side and trim to 24 1/2" square.

ASSEMBLING THE QUILT

Sew the Ivory Tonal 1 1/2" x 24 1/2" borders to sides of quilt. Sew the remaining Ivory Tonal borders to top/bottom of quilt. Press all seams toward borders.

2. Sew the Green & Red 26 1/2" long borders to sides of quilt. Sew the remaining Green & Red borders to top/bottom of quilt. Press all seams toward outside edge of quilt.

FINISHING

1. Layer backing, batting, and quilt top. Quilt as desired.

2. Trim backing and batting even with quilt edge.

3. Use the Red Tonal 2 1/4" binding strips to finish the quilt.

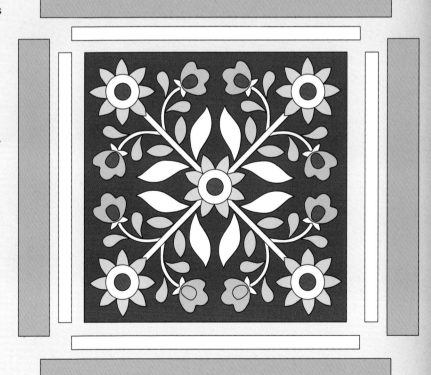

Quilt Assembly Diagram

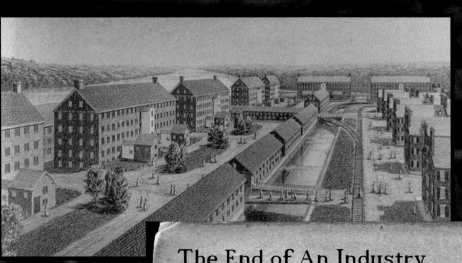

The End of An Industry

Abbott Lawrence, John Amory Lowell and Nathan Appleton incorporated the Boott Cotton Mills, located in Lowell, Massachusetts, in 1835 for the purpose of producing "drillings, sheetings, shirtings, linens, fancy dress goods, and yarns." Between 1836 and 1839, four mill buildings were built along the Merrimack River, each operating independently from the other. A three-story counting house located in front of the mills housed the administrative and accounting functions. The complex grew during 1846 and 1847 with the addition of a fifth mill. A central picker house was added in 1860 and a cotton storehouse in 1865. Mill #6, built in 1871-72, not only contained carding, spinning and weaving machinery; it included a blacksmith shop, a large machine shop, a paint shop and carpenter shop.

By the 1870s, Boott Cotton Mills shifted to a variety and order mill with the six mills working as a unified plant. At the same time, management made the decision to increase production, keep pay rates low, and avoid reinvestment in plant and equipment. This policy ultimately led to the demise of the company. An aging plant with a low paid, dissatisfied workforce had difficulty competing with the South after 1880, when it became increasingly competitive with the long-established northern textile mill industry. However, throughout the 1880s and 1890s, the Boott paid consistent dividends and its stock price remained high.

In February 1905, the mill closed and the corporation ceased. The plant and its assets were sold for $300,000 to a group of investors from Lowell and Boston. Renamed Boott Mill, this new company reorganized management and production, invested in new equipment and retrained workers. Remarkably, the company managed to successfully withstand the economic strains of two world wars and the depression years. However, the bad market and big inventories that existed for cotton textiles during the early 1950s hastened the end of many mill operations in the northeast. Boott Mill became one of the casualties and ended operations in 1955 after one-hundred-twenty years of textile manufacture.

Today, the Boott Cotton Mills Museum, a part of Lowell National Historical Park, pays homage to the mill and the mill tradition of Lowell. With its exhibits featuring authentic mill equipment, the museum allows visitors to experience factory life and the boarding-house experience that dominated the day-to-day world of the Mill Girls.

Boott Mills

FINISHED QUILT SIZE: 43" x 55"
FINISHED BLOCK SIZE 12" x 18"/4; MAKE 4 BLOCKS
DESIGNED, STITCHED, AND QUILTED BY NANCY RINK

Boott cotton mill circa, 1850

FABRIC REQUIREMENTS

Style numbers refer to *The Mill Girls: 1830-1850*
by Judie Rothermel for Marcus Fabrics

1/2 yard Tan & Blue floral print 4423-0150 for block background
  and border
5/8 yard Green Print 4157-0116 for blocks and appliqué border
3/4 yard Red & Blue Plaid 4161-0150 for blocks and binding
1/2 yard Red Plaid 4160-0111 for blocks and appliqué border
1-1/2 yards Cream & Blue Floral 4154-0150 for border
1-7/8 yards Blue Floral 4151-0150 for sashing and borders
3 yards for backing

SUPPLIES

Bias Press Bars
16 – 5/8" to 3/4" diameter buttons OR *Perfect Circles*® by
Karen Kay Buckley for appliqué circles
Thread to match appliqué patches
Air erase pen

Note: Boott Mills was constructed using the freezer paper
and starch appliqué method. The following supplies are
recommended if you plan to use the same method.

Freezer Paper
Mary Ellen's Best Press
  Liquid Starch
Artist's Brush
Mini-Iron
Awl/Chopstick
Fabric Glue

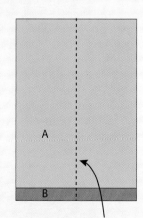

Crease through vertical
center to create placement
guide for appliqué

CUTTING DIRECTIONS

Use Factory templates from Block One on pages 81-86
Use Leaf template G on page 93
Use circle template F on page 96

From the Tan & Blue print, cut: 4 – 8 1/4" x 12" C rectangles; 4 –
  5 1/2" G squares
From the Green Print, cut: 4 –12 1/2" x 1 3/4" B rectangles; 1 –
  16" square; 30 to 36 – Leaves
From the Red & Blue Plaid, cut: 6 – 2 1/4" x WOF strips for binding; 4 – Factory Roofs
From the Red Plaid, cut: 4 – Factories; 8 – Factory Chimneys; 9 –
  1 1/2" F squares; 4 – 3 1/2" H squares; 16 to 20 -- Circles
From the Cream & Blue Floral, cut: 4 – 12 1/2" x 17 1/4" A rectangles; 2 – 5 1/2" x 27 1/2" top/bottom borders; 2 – 5 1/2" x
  39 1/2" side borders
From the Blue Floral, cut: 5 – 1 1/2" x WOF strips, recut into 6 – 1
  1/2" x 12 1/2" D strips and 6 – 1 1/2" x 18 1/2" E strips; 2 – 3
  1/2" x 37-1/2" top/bottom borders; 3 – 3 1/2" x WOF strips,
  pieced together end-to-end and recut into 2 – 3 1/2" x 49 1/2"
  side borders
From the backing, cut: 1 – 51" x WOF panel; 2 – 20" x WOF
  strips; 1 – 9" x WOF strip for hanging sleeve

SEWING INSTRUCTIONS

BOOTT MILL BLOCK

1. Sew together a Cream & Blue Floral A rectangle and a Green Print
   B rectangle. Press seam open. Repeat for a total of four blocks.

2. Fold and crease vertically to create a placement guide line for
   appliqué.

3. Appliqué a Factory to a Tan & Blue print C rectangle. If using
   freezer paper, remove the freezer paper factory template before
   appliquéing factory to block.

4. Position the Factory building, the 2 Chimneys and the Roof
   aligning the vertical centers of Roof and Factory with the
   vertical center of block. Pin or glue appliqué pieces in place.
   Appliqué using matching thread. Make a total of 4 blocks.

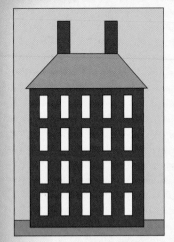

Block Assembly Diagram

ASSEMBLING THE QUILT

1. Referring to the *Quilt Assembly Diagram*, lay out the Boott Mill blocks, Blue Floral D and E sashing strips, and Red Plaid F squares.

2. Sash Rows. Sew F and D patches together alternately to make three sash rows. Press seams toward Ds.

3. Block Rows. Sew blocks together alternately with E strips to make two block rows. Press seams toward Es.

4. Sew together sash rows and block rows. Press seams toward sash rows.

APPLIQUE BORDER

1. Sew the Cream & Blue Floral 27 1/2" long borders to top and bottom of quilt. Press seams toward quilt center.

2. Sew a Tan & Blue print G square to both ends of the remaining Cream & Blue Floral borders. Press seams toward G squares. Sew borders to sides of quilt. Press seams toward quilt center.

3. From the Green Print 16" square, cut 1 1/4"-wide strips on the bias. Join strips together end-to-end to create continuous bias.

4. To prepare the Green Print continuous bias for appliquéing, fold the 1 1/4"-wide strips in half lengthwise, wrong sides together. Stitch a scant 1/4" from the raw edge. Insert the 3/8" Bias Press Bar into the tube, centering the seam. Press seam to one side, trimming if necessary. Shift Bias Press Bar a length at a time until all fabric tubes are pressed flat.

5. The bias vines on the inner border were created freeform. Using an air erase pen, draw vine placement lines free hand. Manipulate the continuous bias tube into position, placing it over the drawn lines. In order to make the vine spiral, spray it with a little water, position it, and then set it with a hot iron. You may need to spritz and iron several times to get the vine just the way you want it. Pin or glue the vine in place as you go. Turn under ends. Appliqué vine in place using matching thread.

6. Position Green Print leaves along vine, and appliqué using matching thread.

7. The quilt shown has red wooden antique buttons that were sewn in place after all of the quilting was complete. However, if you do not want to use buttons, appliqué Red Plaid circles randomly along the vine. Use the 5/8" or 3/4" Perfect Circles templates to prepare circles for appliqué, if desired. Or use the circle template F on page 96.

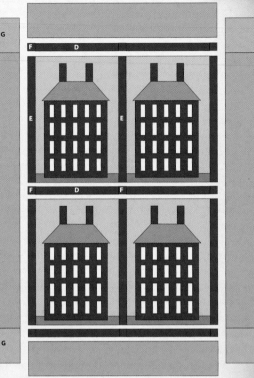

Quilt Assembly Diagram

Bias Cutting Diagram

OUTER BORDER

1. Sew the Blue Floral 37 1/2" border to the top of the quilt. Press seams toward outside edge of quilt.

2. Sew a Red Plaid H square onto each end of the remaining Blue floral print borders, and sew the borders to the sides of the quilt.

FINISHING

1. Sew together the two 20" x WOF backing strips along the short sides, pressing seams open. Trim to 51" long. Sew this backing panel to the 51" x WOF panel, pressing seams open. The finished backing should measure approximately 60" x 51".

2. Layer backing, batting, and quilt top. Quilt as desired.

3. Trim backing and batting even with quilt edge.

4. Use the Red & Blue Plaid 2 1/4" binding strips to finish the quilt.

5. To make the hanging sleeve, iron under ½" twice on each short end of the 9" x WOF" strip cut from the backing fabric. Stitch hem in place. Fold in half lengthwise, wrong sides together. Stitch 1/2" from raw edge, back stitching to secure seams. Press seam open, centering it on the "back" side of the hanging sleeve tube. Center sleeve approximately 1/2" from top edge of quilt back, making sure the seam is against the quilt back. Whipstitch the sleeve in place being careful not to sew through to the quilt front. Leave tube ends open to allow a hanging rod to be inserted.

Starring Judie

FINISHED QUILT SIZE: 99" x 99"
FINISHED BLOCK SIZES: 12"x 12", 6" x 8"
MAKE 48 BLOCKS
DESIGNED, STITCHED, AND QUILTED BY NANCY RINK

In 2012 Judie Rothermel marks her 25th anniversary as a fabric designer. She designed the fabric collection THE MILL GIRLS: 1830-1850 especially for the feature quilt, Away From Home. You may have also noticed that the majority of quilts in this book were made from fabric collections designed by Judie. In fact, my stash is filled by fabrics designed by Judie! Thus, it seemed fitting that I design a quilt paying tribute to her and her contributions to the quilting world as a way of saying, "Thank you, Judie."

The fabric collection featured here is the COCHECO MILLS COLLECTION III, designed in collaboration with the American Textile History Museum located in Lowell, Massachusetts.

FABRIC REQUIREMENTS

3-3/4 yards Cream for background
1 yard Cream Stripe for sashing
2 1/2 yards of Brown Stripe for borders # 2 and #4
7/8 yard Pink Stripe for border #1
2 1/2 yards Brown Floral for blocks, outer border
1/3 yard each of three Dark Pink fabrics for blocks
1/2 yard each of three Light Pink fabrics for blocks
1/2 yard each of two Dark Brown fabrics for blocks
1/3 yard each of three Light brown & Pink fabrics for blocks
5/8 yard Cocoa Moiré for blocks
7/8 yard Pink Moiré for binding
8 3/4 yards large scale brown and pink floral for backing

CUTTING DIRECTIONS

From the Cream cut: 3 – 2 1/2" x WOF strips for strip piecing; 4 – 2 1/2" x WOF strips; recut into 36 – 2 1/2" x 4 1/2" A rectangles; 2 – 5 1/4" x WOF strips; recut into 9 – 5 1/4" squares, cut in half twice diagonally to make 36 – B triangles;

1 – 12 1/2" x WOF strip; recut into 12 – 3 1/2" x 12 1/2" K rectangles; 2 – 3 1/2" x WOF strips; recut into 20 – 3 1/2" H squares; 26 – 2" x WOF strips; recut into 192 – 2" x 3 1/2" F rectangles and 192 – 2" G squares; 3 – 6-1/2" x WOF strips; recut into 48 – 2 1/2" x 6 1/2" I rectangles; 1 – 2 1/2" x WOF strip; recut into 4 – 2 1/2" x 8 1/2" J rectangles

From the Cream Stripe cut: 8 – 3 1/2" x WOF strips; recut into 24 – 3 1/2" x 12 1/2" sashing F rectangles

From the Brown Stripe cut: 4 – 3" x 61 1/2" borders, cut parallel to selvedge; 4 – 3" x 82 1/2" borders, cut parallel to selvedge

From the Pink Stripe cut: 6 – 4" x WOF strips. Sew together end-to-end and recut into 4 – 4" x 54 1/2" borders

From the Brown Floral cut: 10 – 6-1/2" x WOF strips pieced together end-to-end and recut into 2 – 6-1/2" x 87 1/2" borders and 2 – 6 1/2" x 99 1/2" borders

From *each* of the three Dark Pink fabrics cut: 1 – 2 1/2" x WOF strips; 3 – 3 1/2" H squares; 24 – 2" G squares

From *each* of the three Light Pink fabrics cut: 1 – 1 7/8" x WOF strip, recut into 12 – 1 7/8" x 3 3/8" D rectangles; 1 – 3 1/2" x WOF strip, recut into 12 – 3 1/2" H squares; 3 – 2" WOF strips, recut into 48 – 2" G squares

From *one* of the light pinks cut 4 – 4" L squares

From *one* of the light pinks cut 4 – 3" M squares

From *another* one of the light pinks cut 4 – 3" M squares

From each of the two Dark Brown fabrics cut: 2 – 5 1/4" x WOF strip, recut into 9 – 5-1/4" squares, cut in half twice diagonally to make 36 – B triangles; 4 – 3 1/2" H squares; 2 – 2" x WOF strip, recut into 36 – 2" G squares

From each of the three Light Brown & Pink fabrics cut: 1 – 1 7/8" x WOF strip, recut into 12 – 1 7/8" C squares; 3 – 3 3/8" E squares; 3 – 3 1/2" H squares; 2 – 2" x WOF strips, recut into 24 – 2" G squares

From the Cocoa Moiré cut: 8 – 2" x WOF strips, recut into 160 – 2" G squares; 4 – 3 1/2" H squares

From the Pink Moiré cut: 10 – 2 1/4" x WOF strips pieced end-to-end for binding

From the Backing, cut: 2 – 107" x WOF panels; 3 – 25" x WOF strips, pieced together end-to-end and trimmed to 107" long.

Judie Rothermel

Judie Rothermel was the first to design reproduction fabrics for the quilting industry, starting with *THE CENTENNIAL COLLECTION*, for Marcus Fabrics (then "Marcus Brothers") in 1987. With this collection, quilters were finally able to recreate antique quilts with historic significance and accuracy. As any quilting authority would agree, this is a category that can't be ignored in today's quilting world.

In addition, she is the originator of 1930's reproduction fabrics for quilters, introducing the still popular *AUNT GRACE* brand in 1992. Many designers and manufacturers have reinterpreted the look over the years, to the extent that the term "Aunt Grace" has become synonymous with the 1930's print category.

Judie also continues to lend her expertise as a quilt historian in the development of Marcus' collaborations with several museums, including Old Sturbridge Village, which has archived many of Judie's fabrics as a part of its permanent collection. With Judie, Marcus Fabrics also developed design collaborations with the New England Quilt Museum and the American Textile History Museum, among others. These alliances also represent an important segment of the quilting industry.

Among her many achievements, Judie has earned her reputation among the world's best in hand piecing and hand quilting, and she still promotes such traditional quiltmaking methods. Long before she designed fabrics for Marcus, Judie's background as an antique quilt historian, collector, designer and shop owner had already given her a unique insight into the most traditional segments of the market. And she continues to educate and inspire quilters today. Quilters around the globe look specifically for her fabrics when creating a reproduction era quilt, whether it be a Civil War quilt, a 1930's quilt, a turn-of-the-century quilt, or a quilt that represents a particular time and place in American history.

SEWING INSTRUCTIONS

ROTHERMEL STAR BLOCKS

1. Sew a Dark Pink 2 1/2" x WOF strip to a Cream 2 1/2" x WOF strip. Press toward the Dark Pink fabric. Cross-cut into twelve 2 1/2" wide segments. Repeat with the remaining Dark Pink and Cream 2 1/2" wide strips. (*Diagram 1*)

2½" **Diagram 1**

2. To make a Unit A, sew a Cream A rectangle onto a strip-pieced segment as shown in *Diagram 2*. Press seams toward A patches. Repeat to make a total of thirty-six.

Diagram 2
Unit A

FOR ONE BLOCK:

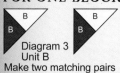

Diagram 3
Unit B
Make two matching pairs

3. To make a Unit B, gather four matching Dark Brown B triangles and four Cream B triangles. Sew together as shown in *Diagram 3*. Make two pairs.

4. To make one Unit C block center, gather four matching light pink D rectangles and a matching light brown & pink set of four C squares and one E square. Arrange patches as shown in *Diagram 4*. Sew the patches together in rows; then sew the rows together. Press seams to the darker fabric.

Diagram 4

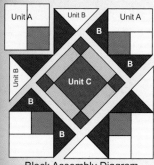

Block Assembly Diagram
Make a total of nine blocks

5. To assemble one block, gather four matching A Units, the two pairs of B Units, one C Unit and four additional Dark Brown B triangles that match those used in the B Unit. Lay out units and B triangles as shown in the *Block Assembly Diagram.*

6. Sew the Dark Brown B triangles to the A Units, as shown. Sew these to opposite sides of Unit C. Sew the B Units to adjacent sides of the A Units, as shown. Sew to the block, matching seams.

7. Make a total of nine blocks in various combinations of the Dark Pink, Light Pink, Dark Brown, and Light Brown & Pink fabrics.

SAWTOOTH STAR BORDER BLOCKS

1. For one block, gather eight matching Dark Pink Gs and one H, along with four Cream F rectangles, four Cream G patches, and one Cream I rectangle.

2. Lay a Dark Pink G square on top of the left-hand side of a Cream F rectangle, right sides together. (Diagram 5).

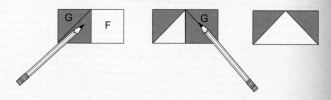

On the wrong side of the Dark Pink G, draw a seam line diagonally from corner to corner. Sew on the line. Trim seam allowance* to 1/4"; flip open and press. Next, place a Dark Pink G square on top to the right-hand side of the Cream F rectangle, right sides together. Draw a seam line diagonally from corner to corner. Sew on the line. Trim seam allowance to 1/4"; flip open and press. Make a total of four matching Flying Geese units.

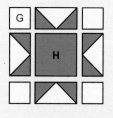 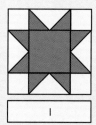

Diagram 6
Sawtooth Star Block Assembly
Make a total of 48 blocks

*Save the triangles for making the Pinwheel Pillow on page 79.

3. Lay out the Flying Geese units along with the matching Dark Pink H square and four Cream G squares. Sew together in rows and then sew the rows together.

4. Sew a Cream I rectangle to one side of the star block, pressing seam toward the I patch (*Diagram 6*).

5. Make a total of 48 blocks using the G and H patches cut from the Dark Pink, Light Pink, Dark Brown, Light Brown and Pink and Cocoa Moiré fabrics.

6. Gather the four blocks made from the Cocoa Moiré fabric and the four Cream J rectangles. Sew a J onto each block to make four Border Corner Blocks, as shown in *Diagram 7*.

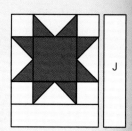

Diagram 7
Border Corner Block
Make 4

SASHING UNITS

1. Lay a Cocoa Moiré G square on top of a Cream Stripe K sashing rectangle in the left hand upper corner, right sides together. Draw a line diagonally from corner to corner on the G square. Sew on the line. Trim seam allowance to 1/4"; flip open and press. Next, place a Cocoa Moiré G square on top to the K rectangle in the upper right corner, right sides together. Draw a line diagonally from corner to corner. Sew on the line. Trim seam allowance to 1/4"; flip open and press. Repeat on the opposite end of the K sashing rectangle. Make a total of twenty-four Sashing Units (Diagram 8).

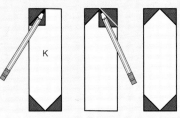

Diagram 8
Sashing Units
Make 16

2. Using sixteen of the Cream H squares and the remaining Cocoa Moiré G squares, use the same stitch-and-flip method to make sixteen Sashing Blocks (Diagram 9).

Diagram 9
Sashing Blocks
Make 16

ASSEMBLING THE QUILT

1. Gather the twelve Cream K rectangles, four Cream H squares and sixteen Light Pink H squares.

2. Referring to *Quilt Center Assembly Diagram*, lay out the Rothermel blocks alternately with the Sashing Units. Sew blocks and Sashing Units together, pressing seams toward Sashing Units. Sew a Cream K rectangle to the ends of the block rows.

3. Make four sashing rows by sewing together three Sashing Units alternately with four Light Pink H squares. Press seams toward Sashing Units. Sew a Sashing Block to the ends of the sashing rows, making sure the Sashing Blocks are oriented correctly.

4. Make the top and bottom sashing rows by sewing four Sashing Blocks alternately with three Cream K rectangles. Press seams toward sashing blocks. Sew a Cream H square to the ends of the top and bottom sashing rows.

5. Sew together block rows, sashing rows, and top and bottom sashing rows.

Quilt Center Assembly Diagram

BORDERS

Border One. Sew a Pink Stripe border to opposite sides of the quilt center. Add a Pink L square to the ends of the remaining two borders. Sew borders to opposite sides of the quilt.

Border Two. Sew a 61 1/2" long Brown Stripe border to opposite sides of the quilt. Add a Light Pink M square to the ends of the remaining two borders. Sew borders to opposite sides of the quilt.

Border Three. Gather eleven of the Sawtooth Stars blocks. Sew them together, rotating blocks as shown. Repeat for a total of four borders. Sew two borders to opposite sides of quilt. Sew a Border Corner Block to each end of the remaining borders, making sure the blocks are oriented correctly as shown in the *Border Assembly Diagram*. Sew borders to opposite sides of quilt.

Border Four. Sew an 82 1/2" long Brown Stripe border to opposite sides of the quilt. Add a Light Pink M square to the ends of the remaining two borders. Sew borders to opposite sides of the quilt.

Border Five. Sew the 87 1/2" long Brown Floral borders to opposite sides of the quilt. Press seams toward outside edge of quilt. Sew the remaining Brown Floral borders to the remaining sides of the quilt.

FINISHING

1. Sew together backing panels, pressing seams open.
2. Layer backing, batting and quilt top. Quilt as desired.
3. Trim batting and backing even with edge of quilt.
4. Use the Pink Moiré 2 1/4" binding strips to finish the quilt.

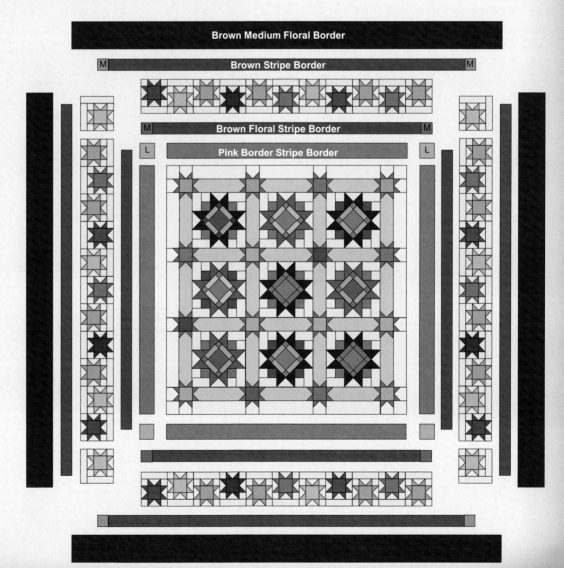

Quilt Assembly Diagram

Pinwheel Pillow

FINISHED SIZE 14" SQUARE

DESIGNED AND QUILTED BY NANCY RINK

FABRIC REQUIREMENTS

This pillow is a "bonus" project made from the fabric discarded when cutting away excess fabric from the stitch-and-flip blocks used in "Starring Judie." If you make "Starring Judie" save your scraps. If not, you will need the following:

6" x 11" rectangle of Dark Pink for flange
1/4 to 3/8 yard total Assorted Scraps of pink, brown, and cream fabrics for blocks
1/2 yard Cream Muslin for borders and pillow back

SUPPLIES

1 –14" square pillow form
1 –16" square of batting

CUTTING DIRECTIONS

From the Dark Pink cut: 4 – 7/8" x 10" strips
From the Assorted Scraps cut: 72 – 2" squares (36 light & 36 dark)
From the Cream Muslin cut: 4 – 4" x 15" strips; 1 – 15" square

SEWING INSTRUCTIONS

PINWHEEL BLOCKS

1. Make half square triangles by pairing a light fabric and a dark fabric square. Draw a line diagonally from corner to corner on the wrong side of the light fabric. Sew 1/4" from both sides of the drawn line. (*Diagram 1*) Cut on the drawn line and press toward the dark fabric.
Trim to 1 1/4" square.
Repeat for a total of 144 half-square triangles.

Diagram 1

2. Lay out four matching half square triangles as shown in *Diagram 2*. Sew together to make one block. Make a total of 36 blocks.

3. Arrange Pinwheel blocks in 6 rows of 6 blocks each. Sew together blocks into rows; then, sew together the rows.

Diagram 2

ASSEMBLING THE PILLOW

FLANGE. Fold the Dark Pink strips lengthwise, wrong side together. Press. Place a flange along one side of pieced pillow center, aligning long raw edges. The fold of the flange should face toward the center of the pillow and the ends of the flange strip will overhang the pieced pillow center. Sew a scant 1/4" seam from the raw edge. Trim ends even with pieced pillow center. Continue sewing flange strips to the pillow center, moving clockwise around the pieced pillow center.

BORDERS. Sew a Cream Muslin strip to opposite sides of the pillow. Press seams toward borders. Trim edges even with pieced pillow top. Sew the remaining Cream Muslin strips to opposite sides of the pillow, pressing seams toward border. Flanges should be facing the center of the pillow.

QUILTING. Layer pillow top with batting. Quilt in the ditch between flange and borders. Quilt parallel lines in Cream Muslin border. Quilt in ditch between blocks, if desired.

FINISHING

Trim batting even with pillow top.

Place the 15" Cream Muslin square on pillow top, right sides together. Pin raw edges.

Stitch 1/2" from raw edges of all sides of pillow, leaving 5" to 8" open for turning.

Turn to the right side and lightly press. Insert pillow form and blind stitch the opening closed.

Template Pages

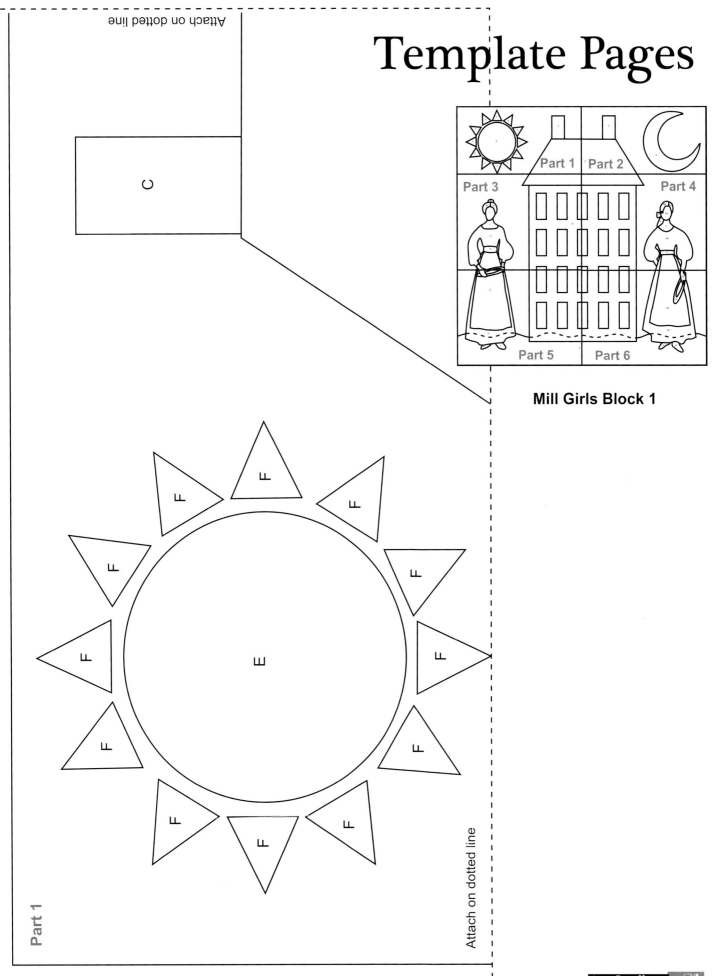

Attach on dotted line

C

Part 1

Part 1 Part 2

Part 3 Part 4

Part 5 Part 6

Mill Girls Block 1

E

F F F F F F F F F F F F

Attach on dotted line

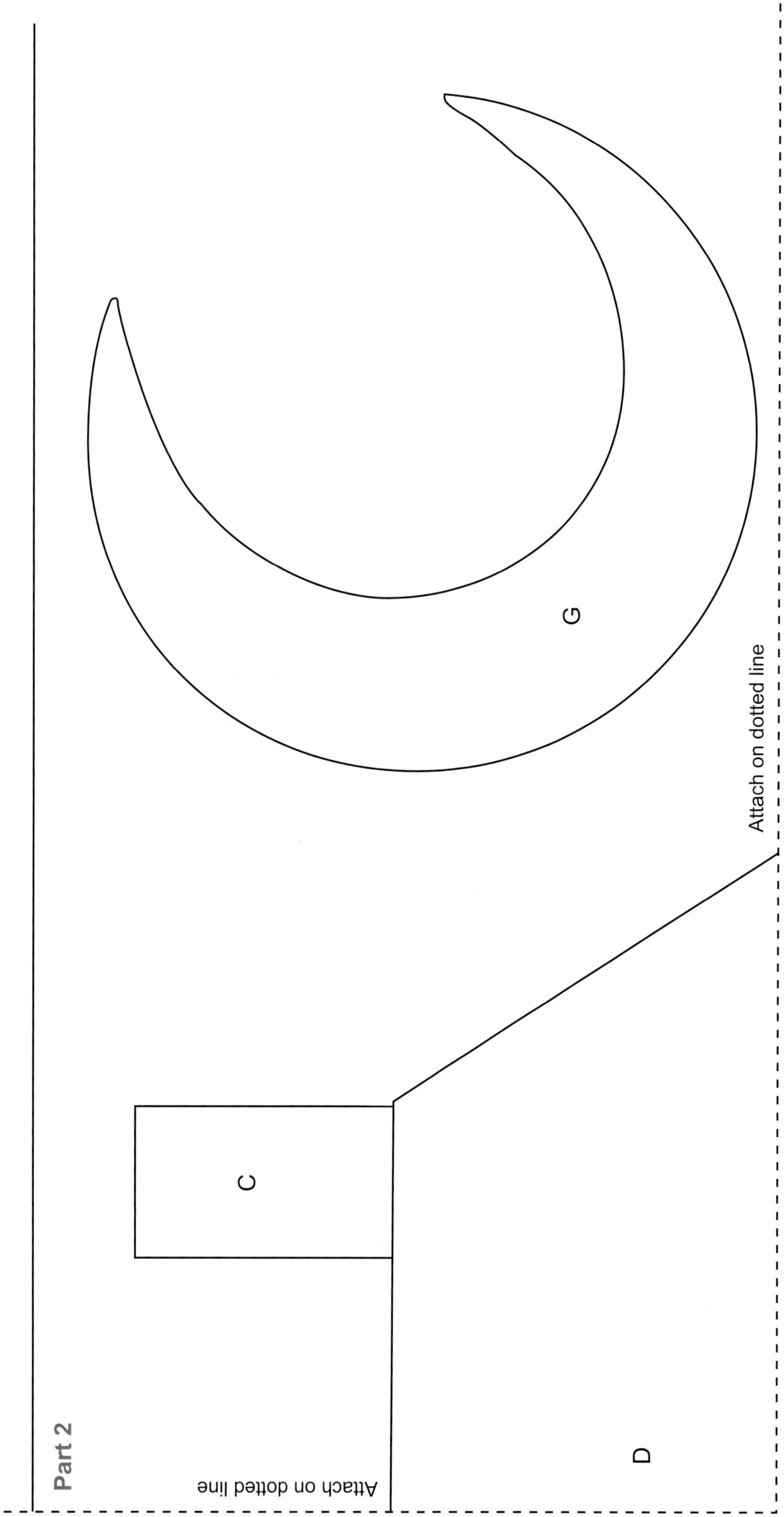

G

C

D

Attach on dotted line

Attach on dotted line

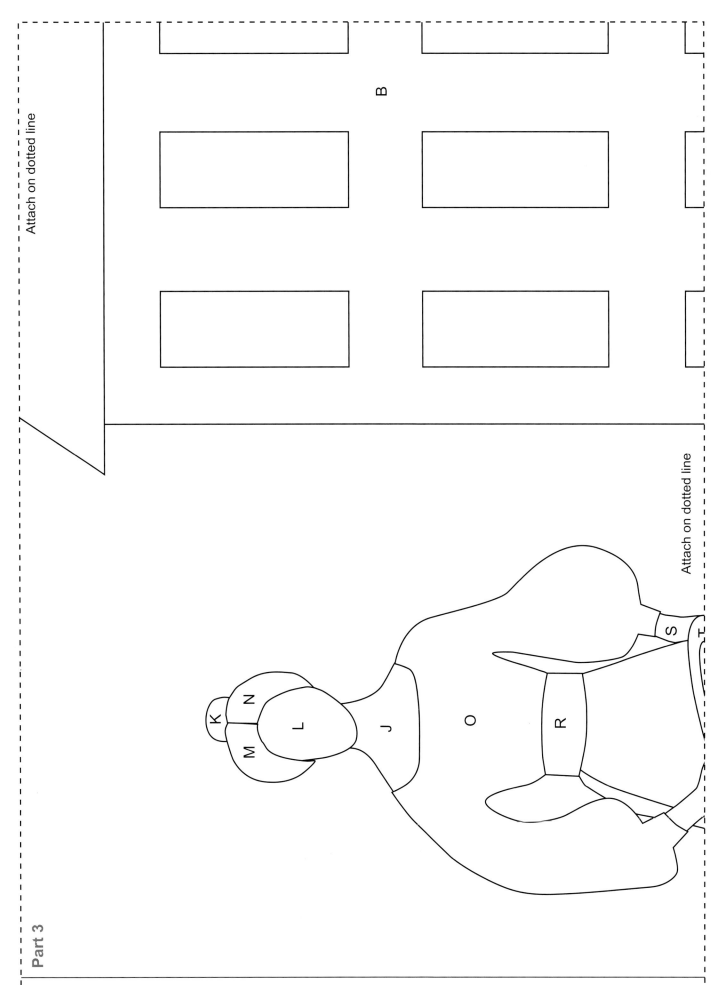

BB
CC
AA
Y
X
Z
HH
II

Part 4

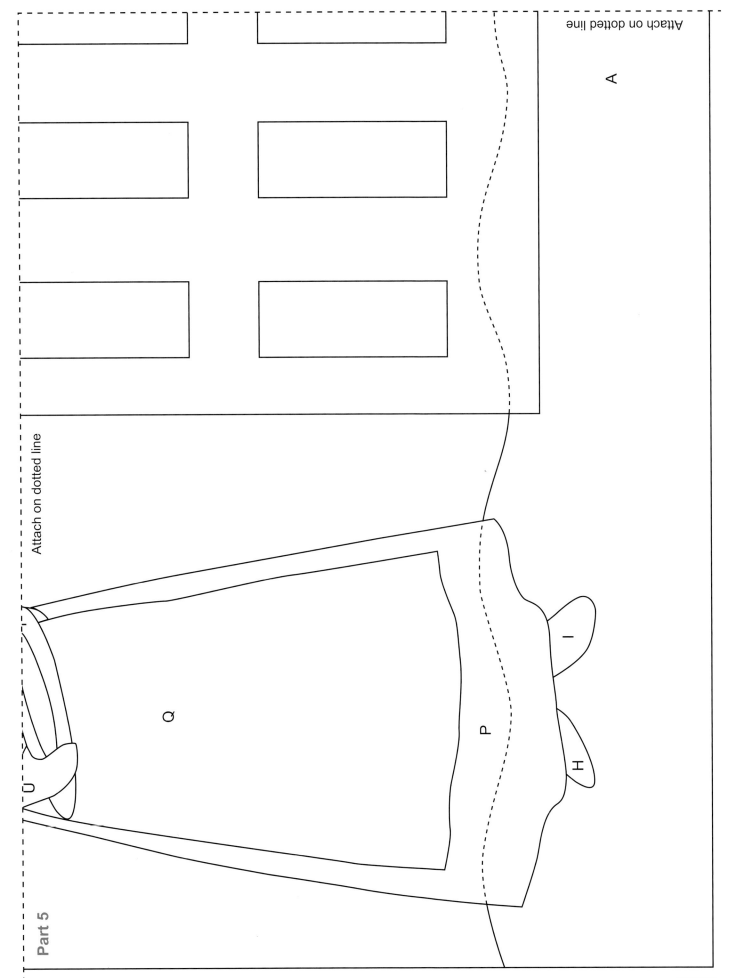

Attach on dotted line

Attach on dotted line

A

Part 5

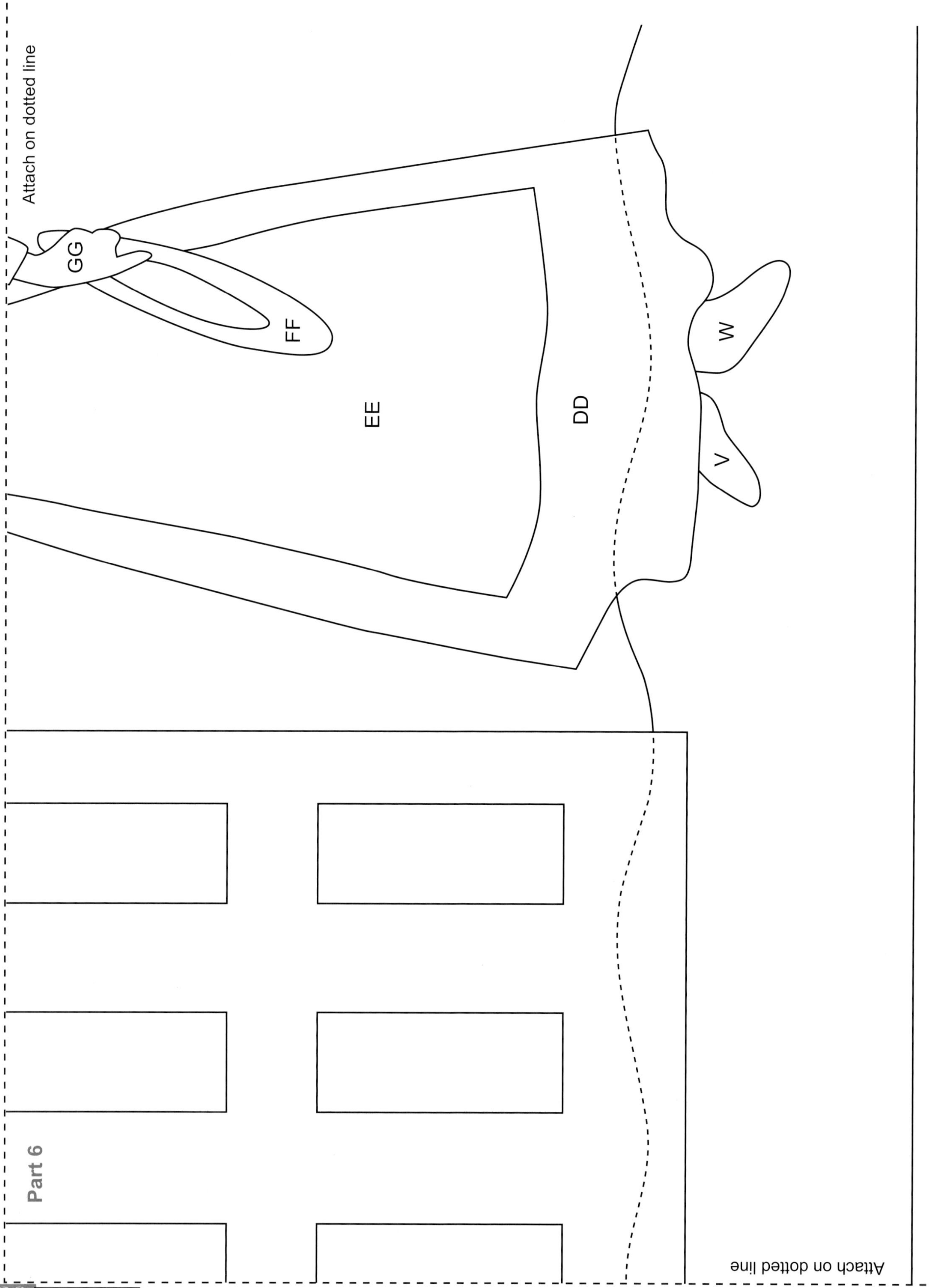

GG

FF

EE

DD

W

V

Part 6

Part 2

Part 1

Mill Girls Block 2

Part 1

Part 3

Part 4

B

Tree 1

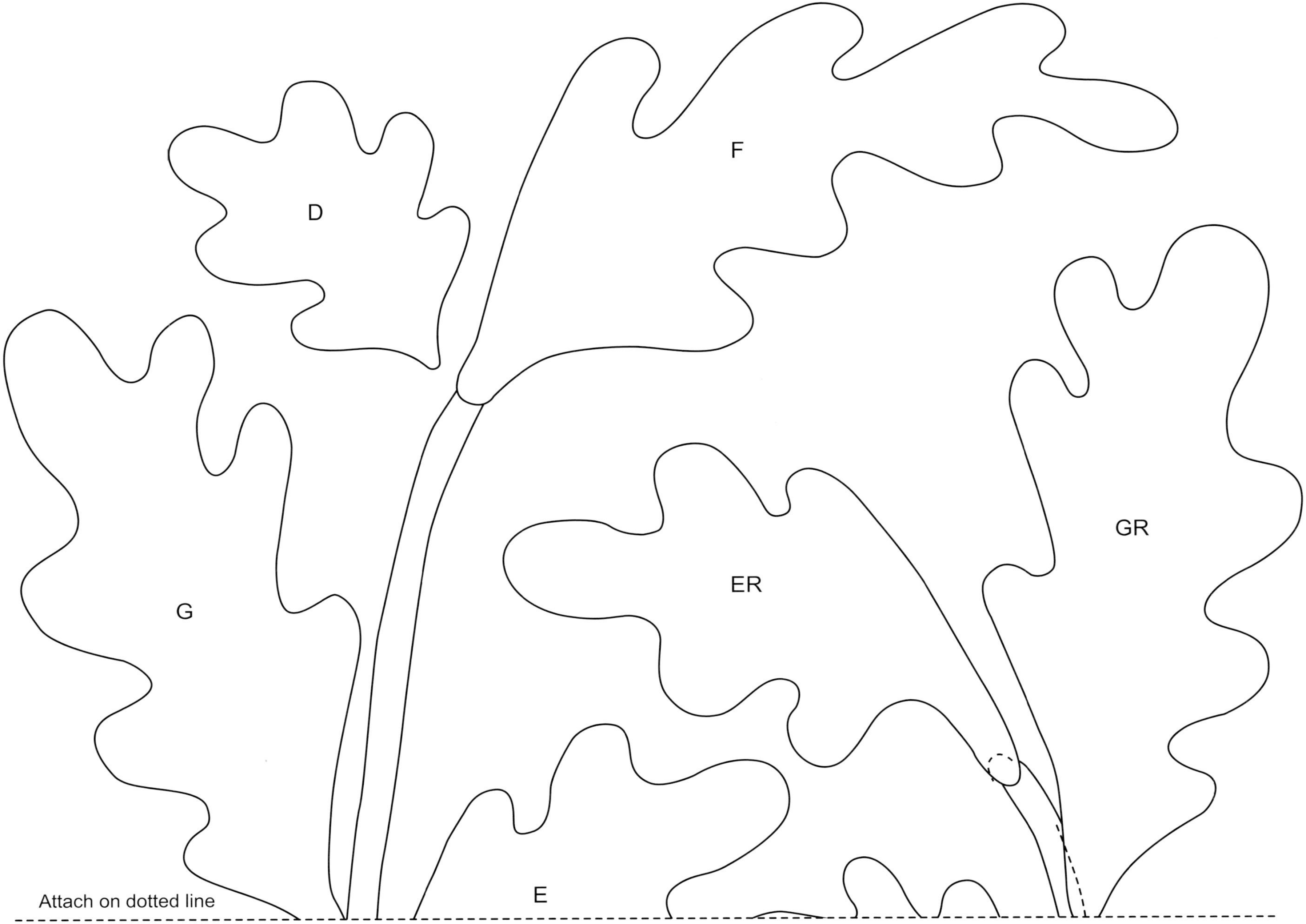
D
F
G
ER
GR
E
Attach on dotted line

Attach on dotted line

Attach on dotted line

C

DR

CR

D

ER

C

CR

ER

CR

Tree 2

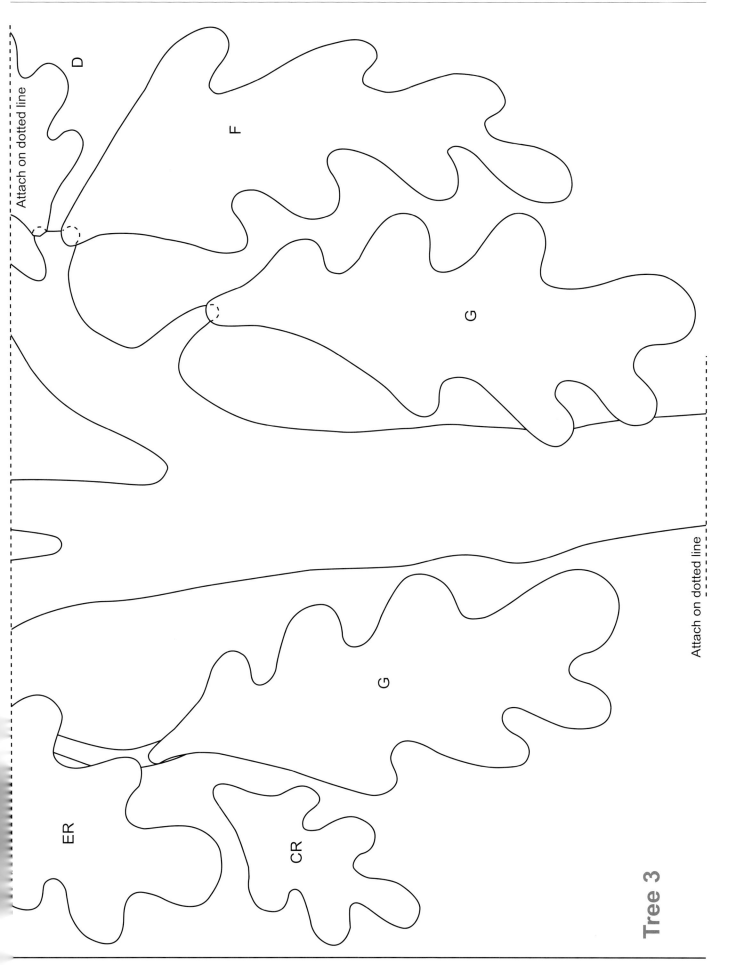

Attach on dotted line

D

F

G

Attach on dotted line

G

ER

CR

Tree 3

Tree Block

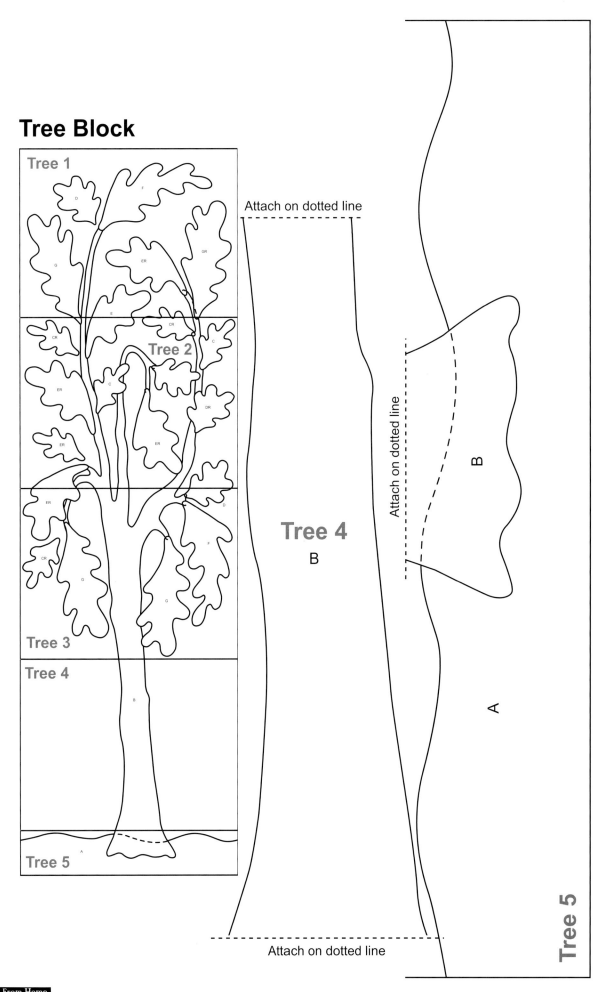

Tree 1

Tree 2

Tree 3

Tree 4

Tree 5

Attach on dotted line

Tree 4

B

Attach on dotted line

B

A

Attach on dotted line

Tree 5

Flower Block 1

B

C

A

HR

H

G

I

I

HR

Attach on dotted line

Attach on dotted line

Flower Block 2

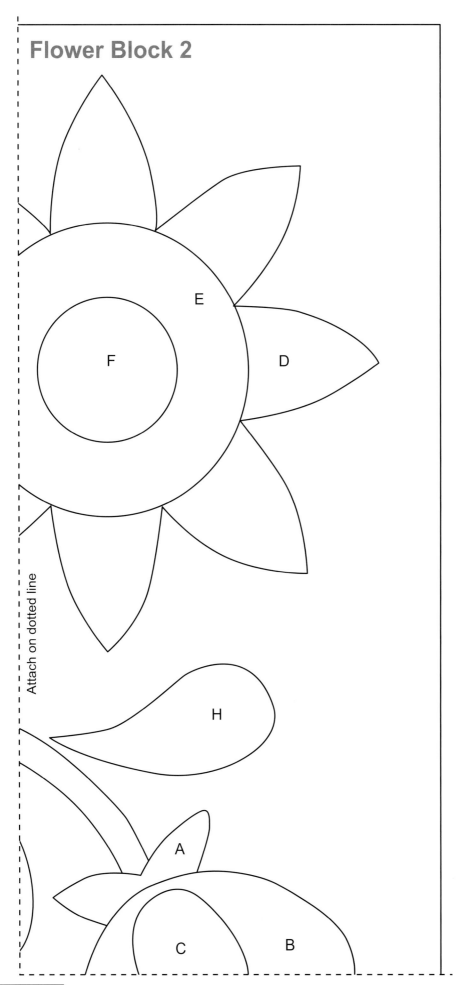

Attach on dotted line

E

F

D

H

A

C

B

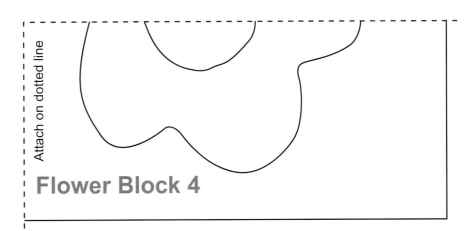

Flower Block 4

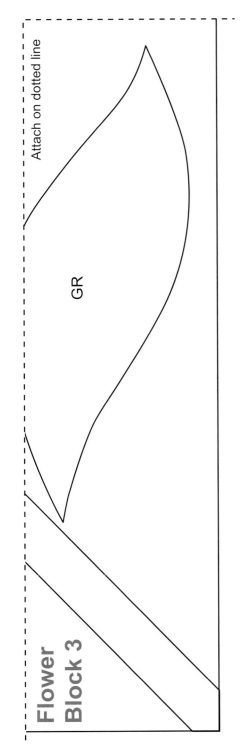

GR

Flower Block 3

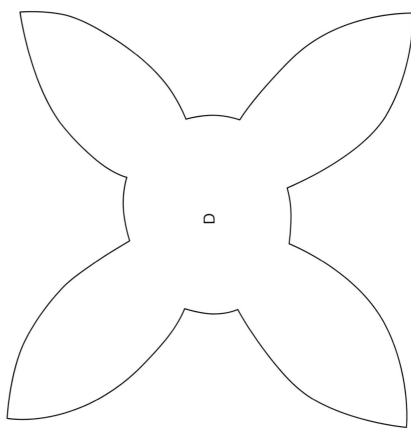

D

Part 2

Part 1

Part 3

Part 4

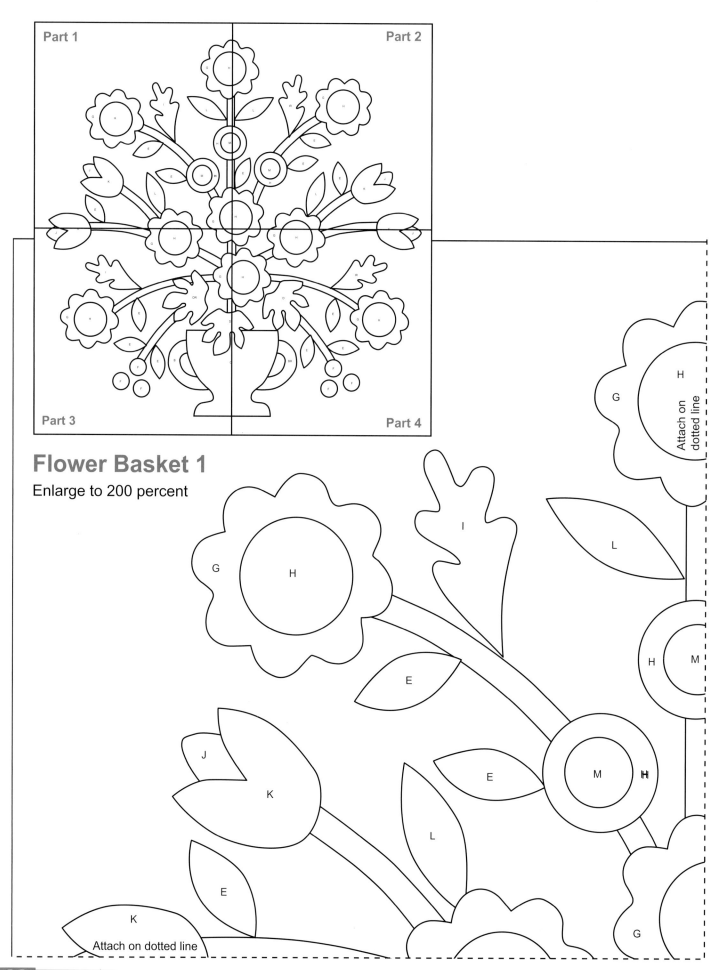

Part 1

Part 2

Part 3

Part 4

Flower Basket 1

Enlarge to 200 percent

Attach on dotted line

Attach on dotted line

Flower Basket 2

Enlarge to 200 percent

Attach on dotted line

Attach on dotted line

Attach on dotted line

J

H

G

G

I

DR

G

D

H

E

C

E

B

E

F

F

F

Attach on dotted line

Flower Basket 3

Enlarge to 200 percent

Attach on dotted line

Attach on dotted line

Flower Basket 4
Enlarge to 200 percent

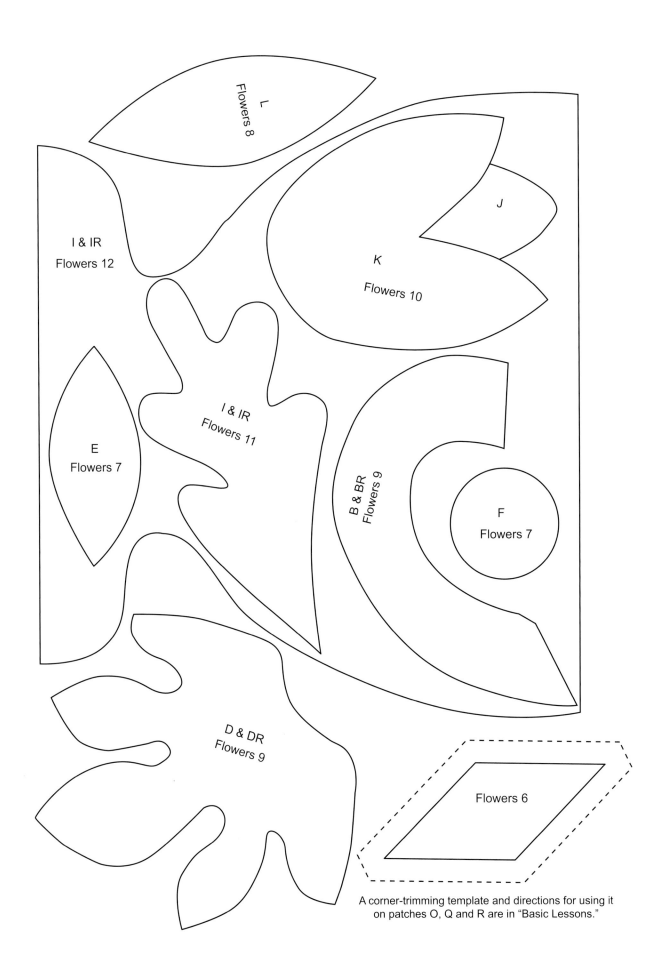

Flowers 8
L

I & IR
Flowers 12

J

K
Flowers 10

I & IR
Flowers 11

E
Flowers 7

B & BR
Flowers 9

F
Flowers 7

D & DR
Flowers 9

Flowers 6

A corner-trimming template and directions for using it
on patches O, Q and R are in "Basic Lessons."

Lovely Ladies

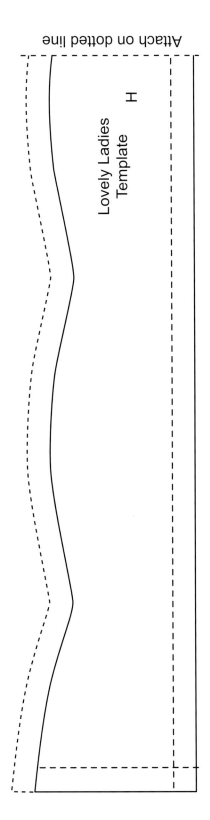

Attach on dotted line

Lovely Ladies
Template

H

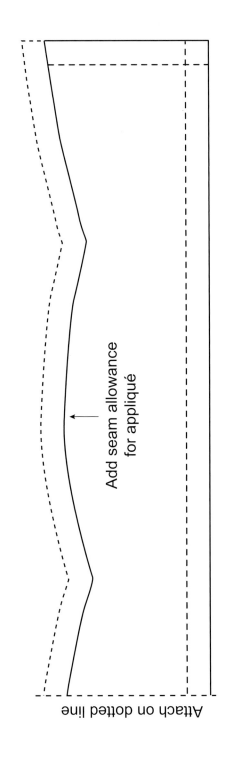

Add seam allowance
for appliqué

Attach on dotted line